What Others Are Saying

"I wish this book was available when I was exploring and considering purchasing a franchise. The information and advice included in this book would have prepared me for the initial issues new franchisees encounter. The book is loaded with sound, practical best-business practices and how to address legal requirements and procedures."

Chad Grubofski, Owner
Mr. Appliance of Mid America, Metro St. Louis

"Franchising is a unique form of business ownership, and potential franchisees have to bring to the table some specific goals, mindsets, and well-thought-out answers to an array of questions. Journey to Franchise Ownership has laid out effective tools for the aspiring entrepreneur. I would encourage those interested in franchising to look at what is presented here. It's good stuff!"

Ben Terrill | Office Owner & President
FranNet of Missouri, Kansas,
Southern Illinois, and Eastern Iowa

"I wholeheartedly endorse Lynne Shelton and her firm, Shelton Law and Associates, for their exceptional expertise in franchise and business law. I have had the pleasure of knowing Lynne for over 12 years, having met her at a franchise conference in Washington D.C. Since then, I have reached out to her and we've stayed in touch. Three years ago, I had the opportunity to use her services for my own business and I was thoroughly impressed with the comprehensive and effective representation that she provided.

I am also honored to say that I have had the distinct honor to read some excerpts from her upcoming book, which solidifies her expertise in the field of franchise and business law. Lynne has a thorough understanding of the intricacies of franchise law, including both the positive and negative aspects of it. She is not only well-versed in legal matters, but also has a deep understanding of the inner workings of businesses, including marketing, accounting, and tax strategies. This unique blend of legal and business knowledge allows Lynne to provide comprehensive and effective representation for her clients. I have had the pleasure of working with Lynne and her professional staff, they are responsive, attentive and always put their clients' needs first.

I highly recommend Lynne Shelton and Shelton Law and Associates for anyone in need of legal assistance with their franchise or business. Her upcoming book is a testament to her knowledge and expertise in this field."

Shane Perkins
Chief Executive Officer
The Ultimate Strategy

"When you invest in a franchise, you are making a long term commitment. You are beginning a relationship longer than some marriages that depends on the same kind of trust and support. Similar to a marriage, it is not a decision that should be made lightly. Anyone serious about taking the first step into a "franchise family" should use this book, filled with great tips from experts of the franchise industry, as a roadmap. This book offers wonderful insight from franchisors on what they look for in an ideal franchisee as well as how to approach franchisors to gain the insight as you complete your due diligence."

Thomas Parks
President and CEO
Premier Franchise Solutions

"Lynne and the team at SLA are truly remarkable at shining a bright light on an often-dim path for budding franchisees and franchisors. Working with them challenges brands to stay ahead of the curve, as they impart a trove of franchising wisdom on their clients' businesses. Franchising isn't easy, cheap, or quick — but there is structure, organization, and clarity in SLA's methods and models to make the process practical and successful."

Victor Schiano,
Chief Operations Officer,
Pampered Peach Franchising, LLC

YOUR JOURNEY *to* Franchise Ownership

YOUR JOURNEY to Franchise Ownership

The Path from Employee to Business Owner

LYNNE D. SHELTON, ESQ.
AND RICHARD AVDOIAN

Go. Franchise. Grow Publishing Co.
Cedar Park, Texas

Your Journey to Franchise Ownership
The Path from Employee to Business Owner
By Lynne D. Shelton, Esq. and Richard Avdoian

Published by Go Franchise Grow Publishing, LLC, Cedar Park, Texas
Copyright ©2023 Lynne D. Shelton, Esq.
All rights reserved.

No part of this publication may be reproduced, stored in a retrieval system, or transmitted in any form or by any means, electronic, mechanical, photocopying, recording, scanning, or otherwise, except as permitted under Section 107 or 108 of the 1976 United States Copyright Act, without the prior written permission of the Publisher. Requests to the Publisher for permission should be e-mailed to mailto:processing@sla.law

Go. Franchise. Grow Publishing Co.
www.GoFranchiseGrow.com

Names: Shelton, Lynne D., author. | Avdoian, Richard, author.
Title: Your journey to franchise ownership : the path from employee to business owner / Lynne D. Shelton, Esq. and Richard Avdoian.
Description: Cedar Park, Texas : Go. Franchise. Grow Publishing Co., [2023] | Includes bibliographical references.
Identifiers: ISBN: 979-8-9895079-0-0 | LCCN: 2023922569
Subjects: LCSH: Franchises (Retail trade) | Entrepreneurship. | New business enterprises. | Success in business. | BISAC: BUSINESS & ECONOMICS / Franchises. | BUSINESS & ECONOMICS / Entrepreneurship. | BUSINESS & ECONOMICS / Development / Business Development.
Classification: LCC: HF5429.23 .S44 2023 | DDC: 658.8708--dc23

All rights reserved.

Special Thanks

First, I thank God, who created the first franchise system model for us to learn from—create a successful model, tell others about it, train them up, and send them off to plant a duplicate in another area where it is needed and/or wanted, thus blessing the people in that area.

To my husband, Steve, who without his support and tenacity, I would have never been a Franchisor, Franchise Attorney, or a good person. His dedication to my mentorship made me into the fake extravert that I can be today.

To my partners and staff, for giving me the time and ideas of what needs to be clarified and discussed in this book, and for tireless and seemingly continual editing and proofreading.

And of course, to my co-author, Richard, for the joint effort and numerous telephone calls, to focus on giving back to the community that we both love a piece of helpful work on how to make that terrifying and thrilling transition from employee to business ownership.

Thanks,
Lynne Shelton

TABLE OF CONTENTS

Special Thanks...ix
Foreword...5
Introduction...9

Section I — Before You Buy A Franchise

Chapter 1 - Passion and Enthusiasm Aren't Enough to Succeed..............13
Chapter 2 - Franchising...17
    What Is Different About Franchising?..................................17
    Taylor-made for Your Motivation.......................................20
Chapter 3 - Doing Your Due Diligence.......................................23
    Terms, Traits, and Tools..24
    Self or Inner Evaluation..25
    Examining Your Personhood Is Key to Effective Leadership...............27
    Good Mental Health Is Key to Personal and Business Success.............29
    External Factors..31
    Next Step - The Numbers...32
    To Read or Not to Read..36
    Negotiation...38
    Advisors..39
    How to Find Advisors..41
    Financing Options...42
    You vs. the System..43
    Proven System...43
    Compatibility with the Franchise System...............................44
    Operational Enjoyment...44
    Cost-Benefit Analysis...45
    Types of Franchises...46

SECTION II — During Your Search For The Right Franchise

Chapter 4 - Attending Planned Meetings.....................................51
    Attending a Franchise Expo..51
    Trade Shows Abound in Educational Opportunities.......................52
    What Education Is Available?..52

  What Type of Person Should Attend?...53
  What Are the Different Seminars I Can Attend?................................53
  Certified Franchise Executive Opportunities 54
  Overall, Why Should I Attend?..55
Chapter 5 - Working with Brokers, Consultants, and Salespeople............57
Chapter 6 - Risk of Investment and How to Mitigate Risk 59
  15 Considerations Before Investing in a Franchise........................... 60
  Additional Resources — Consumer Protection 68
Chapter 7 - Negotiating a Franchise Agreement 69
  Franchisor's Perspective 69
  Franchisee's Perspective..70
  Negotiating Your Next Deal in Advance..70
Chapter 8 - Franchisor Days 73
  Discovery Days 73
  Join the Team Day 75

SECTION III — AFTER YOU JOIN YOUR CHOSEN FRANCHISE SYSTEM

Chapter 9 - Maximizing Brand Value for Everyone's Benefit..................79
  Brand Value 79
  Brand Equity 85
  Brand Value vs. Brand Equity 85
  Using Psychographics to Calculate Brand Equity...............................85
  Brand Value without Brand Equity?...87
  How to Measure Brand Value 88
  The Brand Value Chain...89
  Building Your Brand Value 90
  1. Marketing and Advertising...90
  2. Ambassadorship and Sponsoring...90
  3. Customer Experience...91
  Resources Smart Owners Use to Build Their Businesses 91
  Peer Review Boards 92
  Business Coach...93
  Business Consultant..93
  Assembling a Wisdom Advisory Circle Can Ease Your Mind 94
  Developing Your Wisdom Advisory Circle 95

Chapter 10 - 10 Ways to Capitalize on Annual Meetings.......................97
- 1. Attendance 98
- 2. Location and Timing..99
- 3. Clear Message and Theme 99
- 4. Create Fun and Memorable Moments 100
- 5. Structure Your Program Carefully..100
- 6. Create Excitement 100
- 7. Educate... 101
- 8. Get Involved 101
- 9. Celebrate Achievements 102
- 10. Give Feedback 102

Chapter 11 - Smart Business Practice 103
- Six Pillars for Business Success...103
- Passion..103
- People (Workforce) 103
- Preparation 104
- Planning...104
- Performance..104
- Perseverance 105
- Secrets to Franchisee's Success..105
- Stop Wasting Valuable Time and Energy 107
- Ask and You Shall Receive What Your Business Needs...........................109
- Seek Opportunities to Fail 111
- Are You Doing the Right Things the Right Way?............................... 113
- Goals 113
- Accountability.. 114
- Workforce... 114
- Integrity... 115
- Consistency... 115
- Accelerating Your Business 115
- Dance to a Different Drummer 116
- Mental and Physical Health 116
- Be Current and Always Be a Student Eager to Learn............................ 116
- Establish a Wisdom Circle 117
- Be Persistent 117

  Set Goals 117
  Internal Audit. 118
  What Are You Afraid Of? Delegating Can Set You Free! 118
  Leadership vs. Management — Do You Recognize the Difference?. 120
  Communicating with Impact Makes a Difference 123
  What Makes an Exceptional Manager/Supervisor? 125
  Roles of an Exceptional Manager/Supervisor 127
  Effective Communication Takes an Open Mind, Patience, and Tolerance 128

Chapter 12 - National Marketing vs. Local Marketing. 131
  What to Expect 131
  How Much Should You Spend? 132

Chapter 13 - During the Term. 135
  Why Should You Stay Excited After Year Four?. 135
  KnowledgeYou just think you know it all.... 135
  Benchmarks 135
  Vendors and Suppliers 137
  Competition 138
  What Should Happen in Year Nine?. 138

Chapter 14 - The Renewal 141
  Choosing Nonrenewal 141
  Choosing Renewal 142
  Location 143
  Lease 143
  Refresh 143
  The Renewal Franchise Agreement. 144

Conclusion 145
Appendix - 23 Items Required in the FDD 147

Foreword

As I drive down the streets of my community and see all the recognizable businesses, I can't help but think about how each one represents someone's personal dream. Behind every storefront, or behind each branded vehicle driving to provide a needed service to people's homes, is a courageous, ambitious individual who decided to take the leap into business ownership.

The vast majority of these individually owned businesses, while vastly different in their product and service offerings, share one thing in common—the franchising business model. It is a business model that my husband and I have dedicated our lives to supporting and promoting. You will soon learn why.

My introduction to franchising dates back to my first job with a public relations agency, straight out of college, back in 1984. There, I was assigned to work with a client called the International Franchise Association's "World of Franchising Shows." Through my work with this client, I got to meet and eventually represent franchising greats such as Fred DeLuca, Arthur Karp, and Ron Berger.

I told my husband, Brad, how I was growing increasingly fascinated by the idea of how entrepreneurs could build their founding concepts into national brands through the franchising model. With the encouragement of Brad, as well as my father and other family members, I took the leap in 1991 to start my own public relations firm that would be devoted entirely to helping franchise brands attract new franchisees, as well as help franchisees attract new customers. Over the years, Brad and I have grown Fishman Public Relations to multiple offices and spinoff agencies including Franchise Elevator PR, which specializes in helping emerging concepts, as well as agencies that serve franchisors and franchisees in Canada and United Kingdom. Outside of the business, we have deeply engrained ourselves in the industry through ongoing involvement in the International Franchise Association and other organizations. Brad went on to invest in franchise brands himself and sits on the boards of others.

Through our work in franchising all these years, we have witnessed firsthand thousands of aspiring entrepreneurs who have found a pathway to business ownership through the model. From founders who came up with a solid concept and decided to expand by offering franchises nationally and overseas, to men and women from all walks of life who decided to open a franchise as a way to own their own business, we've come to the conclusion that franchising is nothing short of a miracle of our free enterprise system.

The franchising model allows people to experience the joys and challenges of owning their own small business but with the assistance of an established brand. Every entrepreneur that makes this leap can rely on the premise of franchising: They will "be on their own but never alone." Every franchisee is part of a larger system, but as owners of an independently operated business, they can make decisions to support their local schools and affiliated sports team or the high school drama club. They can do this because they are independent business owners making independent, community-centered decisions.

Franchising is where entrepreneurial dreams are made possible, including my own, but that doesn't mean anyone can just jump right in and expect success. As part of the PR process, we ask new franchisees who just opened their new location to tell us their "why." Many will tell us they were "passionate" about whatever the product or service was. A franchisee who invests in a dog day care franchise because they love dogs won't necessarily be a high-performing franchisee. In fact, they may wind up closing their doors soon after because they realize the business is more about people, customer service, balancing financials, and marketing than about dogs.

By reading this book, you will gain a greater understanding of what it takes to become a franchisee. It will guide you in closely examining if you have the chops to own your own business. It forces you to take a deep look inside and provides thoughtful advice on steps you can take to fill in the gaps where you might fall short.

There are many books about the ins and outs of franchising. But this is the first one I've seen in my career with a "before, during, and after" format that provides a thoughtful, detailed road map for those embarking on the franchise journey. It starts where it should, with a close internal examination, before launching into due diligence of a brand and steps to take after you have made the leap.

Our company's mission is "to increase the number of entrepreneurs and the success of small business owners across North America." Encouraging everyone involved or thinking of becoming a part of the franchising community to read this book perfectly aligns with this mission. Enjoy!

Sherri Fishman, CFE
Co-CEO & co-founder,
Fishman Public Relations

Fishman is a national PR agency that provides media relations, influencer relations, and content marketing programs to generate franchise leads and increase brand awareness.

Introduction

Questions run through your head: How does one go from being an employee to business owner? How do I know whether I specifically can? Do I have what it takes? Who do I know that can give me insight? After I have insight, what steps should I take to get there successfully? And maybe more importantly, what is the measuring stick for "successfully"?

In this book, two experts in their field will share the answers to these questions and so many more. In Section I, you will learn how to evaluate yourself, from a ruthlessly honest place, and what to do with the information you gain.

For those who arrive at the answer that they can become a business owner, this book will walk you through each necessary step of "how to," including how to evaluate your support system and the skill set you will need to begin your trek toward ownership. This book will also discuss the needed fallback plan essential to your success. You need to give yourself the safety net to be daring.

Section II of this how-to book will help you do the due diligence to find out the businesses available and the franchise systems being offered in the industry, how to determine which one might be right for you, and how to utilize the federally mandated Franchise Disclosure Document (FDD) to uncover what the franchisor will do for you for the money you pay them and what you will be required to do for the franchisor if they accept you into their franchise system.

Next the book turns to the ongoing issues of owning a franchise in Section III. After you say yes to joining the system and the franchisor accepts you, you will learn how to maximize your investment and the brand value. Finally, the authors teach you how to determine how long your "ongoing" should be by providing a thorough and effective look at the decision of renewal and the clauses to focus on in a renewal franchise agreement.

This book walks you through from employee to franchisee, with plenty of examples and anecdotes along your journey, and how to take each step on the path.

• SECTION I •

Before You Buy A Franchise

CHAPTER 1

Passion and Enthusiasm Aren't Enough to Succeed

By Richard Avdoian

Startup business owners tend to be full of excitement and enthusiasm. When asked why they decided to start a business, the response is generally: "I have a passion for…"

Passion can certainly be a driving force that motivates a person to leave a job and start a business, but does passion itself ensure business success? No, it does not. Both passion and enthusiasm are significant. They are the seeds needed to create and start a business. But are they sufficient?

Passion will carry a business only so far. If a business depletes all finances and resources before it shows growth and profit, passion begins to dwindle, and pessimism sets in.

Business owners that are overly enthusiastic and lack solid foundation can be driven to exceed their capability to accomplish goals, which may cause an adverse financial outcome, reflect poorly on the brand, and result in a loss of customers and ultimately closure of the business.

It can be costly in wasted time and the financial expense to have "eyes bigger than your stomach"—biting off more than you are capable of accomplishing—not to mention the strain on your mental and physical health, financial future, and family.

Before you take the leap into the franchise world, you need to know whether you are cut out to own a business.

Consider these questions:
- Can you switch from being an employee to being solely responsible for the demands of running a business?
- Do you have the discipline to set and maintain business hours?
- Are you a self-starter?
- Can you adjust to initially working isolated?
- Have you done your homework?
- Is there a need for your product/service?
- Do you have a business plan addressing all facets of purchasing a franchise?
- Do you have sufficient funds to support yourself and your family while you build this business?
- Do you have a clearly defined backup plan if the business is unsuccessful?
- Have you identified your niche markets?

On being the boss/leader, ask yourself:
- Do you have the interpersonal skills and experience to develop relationships and handle the demands of employees, customers, and vendors?
- Do you have the skills to create job positions, interview, and hire and fire employees?
- How confident are you in making decisions?

Business owners are required to make decisions constantly, quickly, and often under pressure.

Are we scaring you yet? Don't stop reading. We promise to help you answer these questions and the following ones as well.

What qualifications do you have to pursue a business? What makes you stand out from the alternative companies providing the same product or service? Today, customers are well-educated and use the internet to Google business owners and companies often before actually making contact. Do you stand out positively in the search? Does your background position you as a leader or expert in your niche market?

To minimize difficulties, create a board of advisors and establish reliable alliances. Don't let your ego get in the way of your success. Business owners who secure the services of business consultants, coaches, networking groups, or advisory boards minimize errors and enhance success.

No franchisee can hire enough people to address all the things necessary to be successful. Rather than trying to do everything, establishing alliances with companies that offer supportive business services can cut costs and bring fresh ideas. So, think long and hard before you decide to open a business—it certainly is not for the faint of heart.

The good news, however, is there is a business model designed to help nonexperienced individuals become business owners. That magical business model is franchising.

CHAPTER 2

Franchising

By Lynne Shelton

You've taken it upon yourself to look into the possibility of owning your own business, and buying into a franchise system is at the top of your list. However, you've encountered the conundrum of deciding which system to buy into. With the myriad options available, the idea of settling on one system can be dizzying and confusing. Furthermore, you may not be aware of how much time you want to invest in the business or what your exit strategy may be. And then, you still have the daunting task of perusing the Franchise Disclosure Documents of the systems you may be interested in, and with hundreds of pages in most of these documents, it doesn't exactly qualify as light reading material.

We will look at each of these topics and how to tackle each one of them and more in this book. We will assist you in breaking down each topic, giving you the information you need to make an informed decision, so you can decide if it is time to "Expand Your Brand®" or "Chart a Course" to another destiny.

What Is Different About Franchising?

Franchising makes up a large portion of the United States gross domestic product per the U.S. Chamber of Commerce. In fact, in the U.S., more than 3,000 franchise systems are actively engaged in looking for additional franchisees in any given year. While many franchise systems were started within the United States, others have been imported into the United States looking for master franchisees to lead the charge on U.S. soil.

When we sit with prospective franchisors and help them to determine whether their existing successful business can become a franchise system, there are 10 things that we have them evaluate about their business. You can utilize the same 10 aspects to know whether a franchise is one that could potentially be for you.

1. First, does it have a teachability aspect to it, meaning is it something that they do that you are capable of learning?
2. Next, does it have adaptability? Just because something works on the beach in California does not mean that it can be adapted to work in the mountains of Montana.
3. Does it have profitability? You should make sure when you're looking at the financials that there is at least a 10% profit margin, at minimum, shown in their historical records of other locations.
4. Once a business becomes a franchise, typically, the franchisor's original locations will always be the least profitable on a net profit basis because they're always using those locations for research and trying out new aspects of marketing, services, and products. Also, once a business becomes a franchise, those locations' profitability can also be improved by better vendor-negotiated deals, which can instantly make the locations more profitable.
5. As a franchisee, usually you will also have access to negotiated pricing from the suppliers and vendors that are mandated under the system.

6. Next is affordability. Is the business affordable for most people to start? And for yourself, ask is this affordable for me to start with my savings and my access to cash or loans?
7. Next, you'll want to ensure that the business is a successful and operating prototype. You want to see it at work not just hypothetically on paper.
8. Does the brand and the owner have credibility? Have they been written about in newspapers, on blogs, or have some form of notoriety associated with the business or the business owner?
8. Is there a differentiation from their competitors? If it's exactly the same as another brand, what is it that will help you stand out? It could be price alone that makes it different, which can work, but you need to make sure you're evaluating that and aware of that when you're looking at the franchise.
9. Next, does the system have sizzle? You know—something that is fun or exciting about this particular opportunity that makes you want to buy it?
10. The next aspect is buyer appeal. Is the system put together well, and is it professionally ran?
11. Last, and probably most important, is systemization. Systemization can make or break a franchisee and a franchise system. The owner can have a successful operating prototype, but if there are not mechanisms in place to systemize what they do, how can it be duplicated it in other places? Does it qualify as the preferable hands-off model, having things happen, as one of my programmers says, "auto-magically"? If not, then you're going to take a lot of time doing things that could be done for you. In our

technologically advanced, things like ordering or reordering products, paying your fees, and cataloging your inventory and security items should all be automated.

When you buy a franchise, you often can sell goods and services that have instant name recognition and get training and support that can help you succeed. However, purchasing a franchise is like every other investment: There's no guarantee of success. Typically buying a franchise does reduce the investment risk by enabling you to associate with an established brand and experienced business owners and operators. They have performed the research and development through many trial-and-error scenarios before franchising their business. Another reason why buying a franchise is a good option is because you get to skip that loss of income and investment by skipping those errors, skipping those advertising campaigns that did not work, as well as the products or services that the consumers decided were not what they wanted or were too expensive for what they got. Whatever the error, it's a franchisor's loss of investment and will not be yours.

Taylor-made for Your Motivation

Franchises can be tailor made to your motivation. Most prospective franchisees that I speak with are looking at franchises for one of a few reasons. First, they are looking for security. They are tired of being upsized, downsized, right-sized, or whatever the politically correct name for it is this year. They want to know that their future is secure, which takes us to the second reason, which is that they like to have control.

The next is that individuals like to be their own boss. There is a huge comfort in the fact of being able to plan what days off you take each week or being able to jump out and go to a family event, a dance recital, or a baseball game or just to plan a family vacation when your spouse or significant other found that special discount deal. Being your own boss also gives you the freedom to pick and choose what hats you want to wear within the business. For example, do you do the accounting for the business, or do you hire an accounting person? Do you handle all the sales yourself or do you hire a salesperson to help with that aspect? Does the business require travel? If so, do you do it because you enjoy it, or can you stop for the time being when your little one comes along? Being the boss affords you all the opportunity to be flexible about which hats you're wearing but also which ones to take off and put on as your life situations change.

Finally, your motivation may be a financial one. Maybe you're hoping for a long-term financial gain. Or maybe you're looking for a quick turnaround where you grow the business up quickly, sell it off, and maybe do it again, thus being categorized by me as a "serial entrepreneur," which is okay—I am one too. For some entrepreneurs, the growth and sale cycle is the excitement that keeps them in the franchise game. Or maybe you're just trying to grow long-term investment for your family to leave a legacy, to be able to give the business to your kids or to another family member someday.

No matter what your reasoning is or what motivates you, there are franchise opportunities out there to fit that need. You just need to know where and how to look for them. Next, we will look at how you can do your due diligence to find the right industry or vertical for you to focus on. Later, we will take an even deeper look at how to find the right franchise for you.

CHAPTER 3 –

Doing Your Due Diligence

By Lynne Shelton

Americans from all over the country dream of owning their own business. Many of these people look to franchise ownership as a way to realize this dream while reducing the startup risk and expense. This chapter will provide key information on how to evaluate and buy a franchise, along with the steps of due diligence needed to not only begin your journey of business ownership but also how to achieve it—soundly.

For anyone unfamiliar with franchising, you should understand some of the terminology being used before getting in too deep. This is especially important in this industry because they use a lot of jargon and abbreviations.

First is the term Franchisor (commonly shortened to "Zor"). In your journey to franchise ownership, you will learn that a good franchisor is a successful businessperson who sells a model of his or her success so that others, like you, may reap the benefits of their experience, business savviness, time, financial investments, and even their failures, thereby allowing their franchisees to avoid the learning curve of mistakes.

Next is Franchisee (commonly shortened to "Zee"). This should not be thought simply as the person who buys a franchise and follows the franchisor's rules. You, as one buying a franchise, are more than that. As a franchisee, you truly are an entrepreneur who buys a business from another entrepreneur, the Franchisor, who has created a successful, proven franchise system; creates jobs in their local economy; and has built a career for themselves and a vehicle for their own financial future.

The last term is the infamous Franchise Disclosure Document (commonly shortened to "FDD"). Although it can be an intimidating document, the FDD is a sales and analysis tool that is required by both state and federal laws. The FDD legal document is required by law to be provided to you at least 14 days before the Franchisor is allowed to accept any money or signed agreements, such as the franchise agreement or an area development agreement. The FDD will teach you how much the franchise will cost, what your roles and responsibilities will be, and what the franchisor must do to help you during the franchise relationship.

Now that you understand the terminology used, it's time to look at why you should consider owning a franchise.

Terms, Traits, and Tools

When you are looking at a franchise, remember that you might spend the next 10 to 20 years of your life in this franchise. Prior to making the commitment to devote this amount of your life to this business, you need to do some personal reflection, looking inside yourself, as well as talk with your family and discuss this with friends or trusted colleagues to determine if this franchise is for you.

Self or Inner Evaluation

The first question you need to answer is whether you want to work on the business as an owner/operator or if you are looking for a franchise where you can hire someone to manage it in your place. Many franchises require that you be an "owner/operator," which means that not only do you own the business, but you are required to work full-time within the business. This can also mean being required to attend training and annual conventions, besides dedicating your working hours to the business. In the alternative, some franchise systems allow you to hire someone to be your manager. This option is commonly called "absentee ownership." If you are looking for the absentee owner type of franchise, remember that in almost every franchise, you will have to guarantee the performance of the franchise, which means you should be very careful about who you hire to run your franchised business. Additionally, realize that if your manager goes on vacation, quits, or, heaven forbid, you have to fire them, you will most likely have to step in to run the business until you hire a replacement manager and get them trained. If this could pose a problem with your work week schedule, one option is to always have at least two managers or a manager and an assistant manager who is cross-trained. This will greatly reduce the possibility of you having to step in to run the business temporarily.

Another important question to ask yourself and those close to you is: "How well do I work with others?" This can feel like handing someone a clip loaded with bullets when they already have a gun in their hand, but you need to know the utmost truth. This must be the second question you get answered. Most of the franchises that people are exposed to, such as restaurants and all other retail-type businesses, have many employees and a lot of face-to-face interaction. However, if that is not your strong suit, you need to own up to it so you are not setting yourself up for failure or stress-filed days. There are many franchise systems that allow you to work from home, allowing customer interactions via phone calls or even email. Regardless of your social skills or preferences surrounding customers and employees, there is a franchise that will fit you perfectly.

Another part of your self-discovery is asking yourself, "Why do I really want to own a franchise?" During the various seminars that I give to franchisees nationwide, usually called "A to Zee – Your 5 Steps of Due Diligence," I pose this same question to the attendees. Most prospective franchisee entrepreneurs give one of three general answers: 1) I want to be my own boss, so I am willing to buy myself a job; 2) I want to buy a business that I can control how much money I make; or 3) I want to create a legacy situation, where I can build up the business and then leave it to my kids, favorite charities, etc. These are all great answers, but they only touch upon a few of the reasons. Those that people will not talk about out loud are that they recently were fired, right-sized, down-sized, etc., and they do not ever want to experience that trauma again. Or possibly they have retired yet are bored, or they have reached a certain age where they are too young to retire but old enough that it is harder for them to find a different job that excites them. Whatever your reason, you should know and understand it before you move forward with a franchise purchase to ensure you are making the right decision and that the franchise system you choose supports and allows your choice. For example, not all franchise systems allow you to leave the business to your children. These are factors you must consider when doing your due diligence.

Examining Your Personhood Is Key to Effective Leadership

When was the last time you did an internal audit? I am not referring to a personal or business financial audit, but rather, an audit of your personal dynamics. I refer to this as an "audit of personhood," which involves examining, identifying, and owning your abilities, limitations, fears, and insecurity.

Today it seems the new buzzwords used to describe oneself are "transparent" and "authentic." The question is: Are you really able to embrace and expose your true self?

You may see yourself as an expert, business savvy, and believe you can excel as a business owner, but if you intend to grow your business, you will have to attract and recruit other experts and lead them effectively.

Without a workforce of talented individuals, growth isn't possible. You will need to be an inspiring, motivating leader, willing to expose your own limitations and appreciate and acknowledge the talents of others.

Here are a few characteristics you certainly want to acknowledge, modify, or avoid in order to be a successful franchisee:

- **Indecisiveness. Reluctant** to make timely difficult decisions, inconsistent about following policies when making employee disciplinary decisions, and does not involve key employees in decisions affecting their jobs. Avoids or delays making difficult decisions because of personal insecurity rather than working with a business coach or consultant.

- **Negativity.** Never seems to be pleased with progress, sales, and the way employees and management address tasks. Makes a habit of pointing out only errors or what could have been done better, not from a mentoring/teaching approach but from a judgment/critical approach, and rarely compliments a job well done.
- **Lack of direction.** Easily distracted; lacks focus. Not open to new equipment, business practices, or addition of products or services. Reluctant to make difficult timely decisions.
- **It is all about me.** Leads with an iron fist—"my way or the highway." Thinks, *Is the decision good for me?* Unforgiving, reacts negatively, and rarely, if ever, takes responsibility for role or lack of role in the issue when things go wrong or employees make a mistake—as they do from time to time.
- **Unempathetic/insensitive.** Distances oneself from the feelings of employees. Totally detached from acknowledging how what they say, how it is said, and what decisions are made directly impact the employees' work dynamics and personal lives. Assume they will simply adjust and, if unhappy, will leave the company.
- **I know everything.** Defensive when asked for advice, clarification, etc. Lacks credibility, and employees question whether the leader is current with trends and innovative practices and is able to grow and sustain the business. Employees wonder if the leader is capable of identifying what they don't know

and investing in consultants and training to enhance their skills and knowledge?

Employees leave companies for various reasons, but one of the primary ones is ineffective business owners who lack key leadership qualities. Take a moment to review your work history. What were the reasons you left your job? If you are serious about starting your business, avoid these characteristics and routinely do an internal personal audit to continue your own personal growth while enhancing your leadership ability.

Good Mental Health Is Key to Personal and Business Success

Let's face it: When most of us hear the term "mental health," we first think of mental illness. We think of movies like *Psycho* and *One Flew Over the Cuckoo's Nest* and words like "psychopath," "schizophrenia," and "bipolar." But having good mental health is more than simply the lack of mental illness and is something we all desire, whether or not we acknowledge it.

When we openly verbalize our desire for happiness, love, satisfaction, peace of mind, and a carefree attitude, we are actually talking about having good mental health.

Maintaining good mental health has to do with everyday life—how we get along with others at work, at home, and socially. It has to do with the way effective business owners harmonize their desires, goals, ideas, feelings, and ambition to meet and deal with the various demands and challenges of building a positive workforce and being productive and profitable.

Good mental health has to do with:
- How you feel about yourself
- How you feel about those who work for you, your family, your friends, your customers, and your community
- How capable you are at meeting the demands of daily life (personal and professional)

No defined line distinguishes between mentally healthy and mentally unhealthy. There are various degrees of mental health. No one characteristic can be taken as an indication of good mental health nor the lack of one indicating mental illness.

One way to identify good mental health is to describe mentally healthy people. **Here are a few characteristics of people who have good mental health.** They:
- Feel comfortable in their own skin and about themselves
- Acknowledge and adjust to life and business disappointments
- Are capable of expressing and monitoring their emotions (love, jealousy, anger, fear, shame, inadequacies, guilt, and worry)
- Are aware and accepting of their shortcomings
- Are able to find the time for and be satisfied with the pleasures of daily life
- Are capable of facing, dealing with, and meeting the challenges of life and business
- Apply their best effort to all facets of their life, both personal and business
- Take on problems and challenges as they happen

- Set realistic goals for themselves, their employees, and their business
- Embrace new experiences and ideas
- Are able to express affection and consider the interests and desires of others (family, employees, customers)
- Are respectful and accepting of the differences of others
- Have and maintain personal relationships that are mutually satisfying and long-lasting
- Don't push or shame others for their shortcomings or allow themselves to be pushed around or disrespected

No one is blessed with all the characteristics and traits of good mental health all the time. But knowing what mental health looks like does provide insight into what it takes to develop and maintain good mental health. By doing so, you are more likely to live a joyful and rewarding personal life and lead a more productive and profitable business.

External Factors

Another big question to ask is whether your family and friends will support your decision to buy a franchise. This is a very important question to ask because, statistically, a family-owned and -operated franchise is more successful because each member of the family has a vested interest in the success or failure of the business. Additionally, without the support of your loved ones, you will have no outlet for your frustrations, concerns, or celebrations.

One question that franchisees fail to ask many times is whether the franchise will work in their market. An overexaggerated example of this is that a snow removal business would not make a lot of money in Miami, but a bathing suit retailer might. Many franchises are for sale in areas that the product or service may not work well in, but franchisors will typically leave it up to you to determine that. As the potential business owner, you should research whether this business has competitors or similar concepts in your target market and whether those businesses are doing well. One way you can determine that is to have your franchise attorney do a competitor analysis for you. Or a layman trick is to obtain the competitor's FDD and peruse the Item 19 disclosure section for any financial performance representations, or if that system does not have an Item 19 disclosure in their FDD, you can look at the list of franchisees associated with Item 20 (although it is usually in an attached exhibit in most FDDs) and then call the franchisee close to your target market and ask them financial questions. If you can spend a little extra money, it is also great to hire a marketing company to perform research into your area about the "leakage" for your proposed industry. *Leakage* in a marketing report reflects the number of competitors in a given area as compared to the number of buyers for that product or service, and the distance the consumer is willing to travel for such services or products. This may cost a little more, but it could be well worth it in the end.

Next Step – The Numbers

So now you have looked at different franchised businesses and thought about who you are and what your goals and support structure would look like, but what should happen next? Next, you should read and reread the Franchise Disclosure Document. If you do not understand the FDD and the franchise agreement, then how can you expect to successfully follow the franchisor's model?

When evaluating the franchise, most buyers look straight to the total investment, which can be deceiving. Item 7 of the FDD lists the total initial investment required to purchase the franchise; however, this item gives a range for the franchise investment and only covers the opening of the business plus the first three months of business. In some franchises, this range can include costs for running the business from your home to leasing commercial space, which can vary greatly. Also, there are many franchises that require you to have a specific vehicle, which can greatly change the total investment if you do not have the vehicle already or if your financing terms are not exceptional.

Every franchisee is concerned with the fees. The three main questions that I get regarding fees are: (1) Is the franchise fee too high? (2) What am I getting for the royalties I am paying? and (3) What is the franchisor doing with my marketing fee? We will discuss these three questions in greater detail below. Of course, everyone asks if they can negotiate the fees, but that will be addressed later in the Negotiation section.

The franchise fee is not likely a profit center for your franchisor; it represents your ticket to get into the system and covers the franchisor's costs associated with locating you, training you, and helping you get opened for business. Depending on the franchise, you can expect to pay typically between $19,000 and $50,000, with the average franchise fee being around $35,000 now. This franchise fee is what the franchisor uses to rent space to train you, pay trainers, cover printing expenses and costs of meals during your training, pay salespeople or franchise brokers' commissions, etc. Most franchisors expect this fee to be used almost entirely on the above expenses and as a payment to cover the costs associated with finding you.

The next expense franchisees ask about are the royalties. Royalties are always an area of contention between franchisors and franchisees. Every franchisee at some point argues that they are paying high royalties and not getting enough support for it. It is best to think of a royalty as your association dues—the payment to continue using the franchise name, buying power, reputation, and support system. Admittedly, there are franchisors that charge high royalties and give very little in return, but most good franchisors have evaluated their royalties and charge an amount that is reasonable based on the services, research, and development they give in return. When someone buys one of the popular fast-food franchises, they know that people will come and buy food based solely on the name; however, what most franchisees do not consider is that the famous fast-food chains have spent a lot of money negotiating with suppliers of the various food products to reduce prices to the franchisees to save them money. Good franchisors will continue to look for ways to make the lives of their franchisees better and more profitable in order to earn the continuing royalty.

Another type of fee that franchisees look at many times is the two typical but separate marketing fees. These are the local marketing fees and the national marketing fees. Almost all franchisors require a national or regional marketing fee, aka the business branding fund fee. This fund should reside in a separate franchisor bank account that the franchisee pays into, typically between 1% to

4% of gross sales, for marketing on a nationwide or regional scale. Many times, franchisees will not see their bottom line increase and therefore argue that they are not getting any benefit from the national or regional marketing. If the franchisee is the sole franchise owner in a state, then this may be temporarily true, but in most instances, franchisees will experience some exposure in their general area from the national or regional marketing fund. A national or regional marketing fund should be supplemented with your local marketing efforts. Franchisors will often require that franchisees spend a minimum amount in their local territory. These amounts can vary from franchise system to franchise system but normally run between 3% and 10% or, in some franchises, can be a flat monthly, quarterly, or annual amount. Local marketing can be used in many ways, including sponsoring local adult or Little League sports teams, TV commercials, radio, newspapers, door hangers, and even combined with other franchisees to create a cooperative advertising budget where franchisees operating in a particular area all pool their funds and buy a bigger ad that names all of the franchisees' locations. Franchisees should always talk with the franchisor, other franchisees, or marketing companies to determine what type of local marketing works best for their brand.

There are many other areas of the FDD and other fees that could be explained. Make sure you talk about all the fees with your franchise attorney. All fees are spelled out in the FDD, so let's turn our attention specifically to that beast of a document.

To Read or Not to Read

There is a disturbingly surprising number of franchise buyers who do not read the Franchise Disclosure Document (FDD) or franchise agreement before buying a franchise. This leads to franchisees who are ignorant of the contractual obligations that they have committed themselves to and end up filing frivolous lawsuits later during their term or constantly are complaining that the franchisor is not doing something that can be easily explained by reading the franchise agreement. Alternatively, other franchisees read through the franchise documents but do not talk with a third party who is knowledgeable about franchising. After talking with many of these franchise buyers, I have found two reasons that people do not talk with their advisors. The first reason is that they feel there is nothing that they could do about the franchise agreement anyway (because the franchise salespeople are very good at telling you this), and the second reason is that they do not have the money to hire someone to review the documents (in which case, you should not buy a franchise yet).

Without stretching the truth, most franchise agreements can be negotiated to a point. Many franchisors will tell buyers emphatically that they do not negotiate, which many times will stop a buyer from talking with an attorney or CPA because they think the terms are set in stone. What many franchise buyers do not realize is that if they take a different approach and work with a qualified franchise attorney, many of these franchisors will move at least a little on some of the more important details that do not harm the franchise system.

Every FDD must contain 23 items that must be disclosed by every franchisor. They are required to contain certain information in each item if it is true of a particular franchise brand. The required topics for the 23 items must be exactly as the Federal Trade Commission states and are shown in a table of contents with the starting page number for that topic at the beginning of the FDD (within the first few pages). We have omitted the page numbers below and are just reflecting the titles of these items for your reference. The required items are:

Item 1: The Franchisor, and Any Parents, Predecessors, and Affiliates
Item 2: Business Experience
Item 3: Litigation
Item 4: Bankruptcy
Item 5: Initial Fees
Item 6: Other Fees
Item 7: Estimated Initial Investment
Item 8: Restrictions on Sources of Products and Services
Item 9: Franchisee's Obligations
Item 10: Financing
Item 11: Franchisor's Assistance, Advertising, Computer Systems, and Training
Item 12: Territory
Item 13: Trademarks
Item 14: Patents, Copyrights, and Proprietary Information
Item 15: Obligation to Participate in the Actual Operation of the Franchise Business
Item 16: Restrictions on What the Franchisee May Sell

Item 17: Renewal, Termination, Transfer, and Dispute Resolution
Item 18: Public Figures
Item 19: Financial Performance Representations
Item 20: Outlets and Franchisee Information
Item 21: Financial Statements
Item 22: Contracts
Item 23: Receipt

Negotiation

A general rule is that franchisors do not want to set a trend for future franchise buyers to negotiate dollars and percentages. This is because if a franchisor discounts a royalty fee, marketing fee, or the initial franchise fee, then they have to disclose that negotiation in the FDD or through special filings with the state attorney general's office, or other governmental agency, where future franchise buyers may see it. This creates the trend that future franchise buyers want to get the same deal that the other buyer received, which has led many franchisors to have their take-it-or-leave-it mentality.

The key to negotiating is to know what is most valuable to you and your situation. If leaving a business for your family is important, then focus on those provisions. If you are interested in having a larger territory, then think about the give-and-take that you can work with to acquire the larger territory, which does not always mean paying twice the franchise fee for twice the territory. Everyone wants to pay lower fees, but that is not going to happen for most franchise systems. However, before you start negotiating, you need to thoroughly complete your due diligence, and advisors can help.

Advisors

Some franchise buyers do not talk with advisors because they feel advisors will cost too much. Before talking about cost, the first step is to know who your advisors are. Many of these advisors do not cost anything but time. Advisors consist of family, friends, franchise brokers, the franchisor, and franchisees, which cost no more than some time to call them and maybe buy them lunch. Other advisors cost money, such as accountants and attorneys, but considering the overall investment for a franchise and the possible problems that could occur without someone giving you great advice, the cost of an attorney or accountant is minimal.

Family and Friends

When talking with friends and family, ask them what type of business they think you should be in and then talk with them about the prospective franchise purchase. In most cases, friends and family know you better than you think and can give great suggestions. The other benefit to having friends and family on your side is that they give a support structure that allows you to vent to on bad days and celebrate with on good days.

Franchise Brokers and Consultants

Franchise brokers are typically independent salespeople who work for many different franchise systems. Franchise consultants are most often salespeople who work in-house for a franchise system.

Talking with franchise consultants and franchise brokers is a great way to learn about various types of franchises. Many franchise brokers will give you multiple franchise options to evaluate, which can be "out of the box" for your skill set but could be very well tuned to your personality type and financial resources. We will discuss this in greater detail in an upcoming chapter.

Franchisor and Franchisees

In addition, the franchisor and franchisees are a great resource. During a Discovery Day, there are opportunities to talk with the franchisor's staff about different points, and talking with franchisees will give any buyer the opportunity to learn about the day-to-day life of a franchisee, which can be very valuable information.

Accountants

The next type of advisors are the advisors that require payment. Accountants and attorneys are valuable sources of information related to the franchise. Talking with accountants can help any buyer understand the financial performance representations of the franchise (i.e., the "how much do franchisees make?" representations) and can help franchise buyers understand what their financial limitations are for that particular business, which we will discuss later in more depth.

Franchise Attorneys

Having an attorney review the franchise agreements is a big step that some misguided franchise buyers skip. When talking with an attorney about the franchise agreement, the key is to find an attorney that specifically works in franchising. Most people see the franchise agreement as a contract, but what they do not know is that there are special rules that apply to franchising that do not apply to other areas of law. This means that, yes, your business attorney could review the franchise agreement, but they may, and probably will, advise you improperly and miss some of the areas that are interpreted under franchise law. Talking with an attorney does not need to be costly either. Most franchise attorneys, whether they charge a flat rate or hourly, will bill somewhere around $2,500 to $3,500 to review the franchise documents. This cost compared to the average $300,000 or more total franchise investment is a small price to pay to understand what the obligations of both parties are under the franchise agreement. And don't forget to have your franchise attorney also review the letter of intent (LOI) if you have one and the lease agreement if you are going to be open to the public. The lease, if you have one, will be your most expensive contract, far more even than your franchise agreement, and thus it deserves the legal review as well. There are franchise-specific terms and clauses that you want to be contained within the franchise location lease agreement that are not going to be there with any standard landlord lease agreement. The clauses protect not only you, but also the franchise brand as a whole, and can ensure you are not overrun by competitors in your shopping plaza.

How to Find Advisors

Researching franchise attorneys, accountants, or financial lenders can be easy. With organizations such as the International Franchise Association, research can be done through their website to discover different advisors who focus on franchising. Additionally, with publications like *Franchise Connect*, you can find advisors who are at the forefront of the franchise industry and want to help.

Financing Options

Finally, let's discuss financing the franchise purchase. When looking at financing, every franchise buyer needs to ensure they have enough money to not only cover the franchise purchase but also to cover their living expenses and employee salaries for anywhere from a few months to a year or more. Over the last several years, everyone has learned that acquiring financing has become harder, but what most people have not realized is that financing for franchise purchases has been better than most. The reason franchise purchases are getting financing are the same reasons I have shown why franchising is a great way to own a business. Banks and other lending institutions see the value within different franchises and often can be given financial documentation from the franchisor to assist with the application process.

There are alternatives to bank loans as well. Companies have appeared across the U.S. to help people tap into their retirement accounts to finance their franchise purchase. Before approaching one of these companies, research them. When rolling over an IRA or 401(k), many rules must be followed to avoid penalties with the IRS, so be sure to thoroughly research the company before working with them. Also pay attention to the ongoing fees; you should not have to pay more than around $150 per year to maintain the account after it has been rolled over.

Now that you know more about yourself and what advisors will help with your due diligence, let's compare you verses the system.

You vs. the System

Many people do not understand the power of franchising. Franchising as an industry does more for the U.S. economy and job rate than any other industry. Although helping the economy and job rate is a noble cause, most people go into business for themselves to be their own boss, to have job stability, or to build something to benefit themselves and their families. Franchising is a great vehicle to make this happen.

During your search for a franchise, you should remember three rules: First, make sure the franchisor really does have a proven system that works; second, make sure that you are compatible with that system; and third, make sure you will enjoy following and operating the system for as long as you intend to own the business!

Proven System

One way to determine whether the system works is to talk with other franchisees of that business. By law, the franchisor is required to list the existing franchisees with their contact information, along with an additional list of former franchisees who have left the franchise system within the FDD. You should take full advantage of this list; this is where your due diligence comes in. Contact many of the franchisees and ask them questions, such as what their opinion is of the business; whether they would recommend owning this franchise to others; and if they could do it all over again, would they? And don't forget to ask the follow-up question behind each one: "Why?" For example, if they would not do it again, why not? Their reasonings could cause no trepidation in you at all, such as, "It was my husband's dream, and we got divorced." Those set of facts should not have a negative or an all-stop influence on whether you should buy this franchise.

Compatibility with the Franchise System

With the average franchise term being 10 years, you must choose a franchisor that you're compatible with. How do you know if you are compatible with this franchisor or the franchise system as a whole? You take a compatibility test. A great number of franchise systems have their own franchise personality/compatibility test. If the system that you are looking at does not have one, feel free to take ours from the authors' website, www.SLA.Law, as well as the answers you gleaned from our previous chapters.

Operational Enjoyment

With the average franchise term being 10 years, you must choose a franchise system or industry that operates a business that you will enjoy operating for the full term, that is, if you intend to be a full-time operator of the business, also known as an owner-operator in the franchise industry. If you are not going to be an owner-operator, you should ask yourself if this is going to be a business that you will be proud to own and are qualified to hire the type of managers needed to run the business on a daily basis. However, you should also keep in mind that if a manager quits or is off work for vacation or due to illness, then there is a possibility that you would need to step into the daily operational role until the manager returns.

Cost-Benefit Analysis

With the above rules in mind, you should perform a cost-benefit analysis of the franchise or franchises you are considering. During your analysis, consider whether the cost of that particular franchise is worth it. Look not only at the cost of the franchise fee, but also at the total investment necessary to get the franchise open and operating. Make sure it is not more than you can realistically handle on your own, which we will cover in more detail in our next few chapters.

You must also consider your lifestyle and family in your cost-benefit analysis. Almost all franchises will require that you attend training at the franchisor's location for several days to several weeks, depending on the franchise system. Ensure you can afford to be gone from your family or even your "day job" for this period. Additionally, owning and operating a franchise will bring new roles and responsibilities to your life. During your self-analysis, make sure that you are prepared to handle the additional responsibilities such as bookkeeping, payroll, regular communications with and reporting to the franchisor, hiring and firing, advertising and marketing, the overall day-to-day operations of running the business, and all other roles that may be applicable. If you are not strong in one of these areas, do not worry because many franchise systems will allow you to hire managers to help with some of those roles. The important part is to realize when you need one to help you.

Types of Franchises

Now that you have a general idea of the roles to be played in a franchise, you need to consider the types of franchises available to you.

Within all the franchises you will encounter are two classes of franchises: the business format franchise and the product distribution franchise. Each format requires its own set of requirements and skills. In the business format franchise, you will use the franchisor's trademark, trade name, or service mark and be required to distribute the brand's products or services. You will additionally receive the methodologies and procedures necessary for the successful operation of the franchised business, unlike in a product distribution system. A majority of the franchises that are purchased now are classified as business format franchises. Not as common is the product distribution franchise, which can include gas stations and car dealerships. Product distribution franchises require that you distribute the brand's products and services but normally do not require or may not offer the use of the trade name or the trademark. For example, there is a popular BBQ restaurant in Texas that also contains a gas station selling a popular brand of gasoline.

Most people, when asked to name a franchise, automatically think of popular fast-food restaurants; but what most do not know is that restaurants only account for one of nearly 300 industries offering businesses that are franchised. In the U.S. today, franchises are available in all types of industries, from medical to tax preparation businesses and from doggy daycare and pooper scoopers to senior care, just to list a few. Additionally, some franchises require commercial or retail leases, while others you can run from your home office. With almost 300 different industries to choose from, there is a franchise out there to suit the needs, desires, and skill sets of any would-be business owner.

Ready to say yes? Then keep reading.

In upcoming chapters, we will take these discussions further and give you the tools necessary for further analyzation to find ways of becoming a stronger business owner. Now, let's learn what additional steps are needed to complete your journey to becoming a franchise owner.

SECTION II

During Your Search For The Right Franchise

Congratulations!

You have made the mental decision to go for it! Be proud of yourself and take a moment to pat yourself on the back and realize what all you have accomplished so far. Believe me, no one else is going to pat you on the back. Honestly, some of the hardest work is already behind you.

As Woody Allen is credited with saying, "Eighty percent of success is showing up." You have shown up for yourself and made the decision to become a franchisee and leave employment or corporate life behind.

Now all we have to do is find the right one for you and get it opened. That is exactly what we will walk you through in this section.

CHAPTER 4

Attending Planned Meetings

By Lynne Shelton

O nce you have decided that franchising is for you, you will have the job of deciding which one is for you. There are many ways to research the franchise market. However, as with other relationships, a first-person encounter is always best. There are several ways to get that firsthand experience in franchising. In this chapter, we will look at a few of them. First up is Franchise Expos.

Attending a Franchise Expo

There are two main exposition ("expo") circuits in the United States: a national franchise expo company and a regional-focused expo company.

The nationally focused company is **Comexposium**, which is better known by its previous name of MFV Expo. They typically have four shows at minimum per year. They host a three-day Franchise Expo South typically in Miami/Ft. Lauderdale, Florida, or Houston, Texas. They hold the three-day International Franchise Expo, which is typically in May or June at the New York City Convention Center; a three-day West Coast Franchise Expo typically held somewhere around Los Angeles/Anaheim, California, or Phoenix, Arizona, areas; and then they have been dabbling with two-day shows in Chicago, Houston, or Nashville for the last few years.

The regionally focused franchise expo company is National Event Management out of Canada. They usually have two-day regional shows a year, to the tune of 15 to 18 each year. More shows are presented in the spring circuit than in the fall. Typical locations in the United States include cities such as Dallas, Houston, New York/New Jersey, Los Angeles, Chicago, Virginia/Washington D.C., Orlando, Miami, Minneapolis, San Diego, Atlanta, Denver, and Tampa, although they can vary from year to year.

Trade Shows Abound in Educational Opportunities

Trade shows are always great places to pick up tidbits of information, but within the franchising industry, they especially epitomize their industry: they teach others. After all, isn't that what franchising is all about—teaching others to do what you already know how to do and receiving a fee for that ongoing knowledge? At Franchise Trade Shows across the country, education opportunities abound.

What Education Is Available?

Many people attend these conventions with the hope of finding the "hot" franchise that will make them millions and allow them to quit their current job, but what many do not realize is that the actual "hot" commodity can be found in the seminars rather than just in the exhibit hall. Through the educational seminars, many of which are free with registration, budding entrepreneurs and existing franchisors can educate themselves about the benefits of franchising, the pitfalls to avoid, as well as the steps it takes to be successful. From franchising your business, to franchisor/franchisee relations, to analyzing and breaking down the Franchise Disclosure Document, there is a seminar for everyone to attend and learn from.

What Type of Person Should Attend?

Many times, people think that they don't need to attend the seminars until they have encountered a problem or are ready to pull the trigger. However, that simply is not true. During seminars, you will meet franchisors of all sizes, franchisees who own one or multiple businesses, business owners looking to franchising as a method of growth, and people who are driven to own their own business and see franchising as a way of getting into a profitable business while avoiding some of the hurdles early on.

What most people fail to realize is that no matter your skill set, everyone can benefit from attending the franchise seminars offered throughout the conventions, regardless of whether you have just begun to consider franchising, are at the point of narrowing down what type of franchise you would like to operate within, or if you are currently evaluating your top two or three franchise systems.

If you are looking to buy a franchise, then it would greatly benefit you to take a course on what goes into the franchise documents and how can you negotiate the terms. However, if you are just starting out as a franchisor or are ready to get the ball rolling, you will be enriched by taking a course on operations manuals or franchisee relations.

What Are the Different Seminars I Can Attend?

Education abounds. No matter the type of information you are looking for, you can find the right entrepreneurial seminar at the franchise conventions. From "The As to Zs of Buying a Franchise" for those looking to be their own boss to "The Profitability of Franchising" for those looking to take their business to the next level, everyone will find seminars to fit their budget, experience level, and goals as well as engage with speakers who have the passion and knowledge to answer all of your questions.

If you are looking to purchase a franchise, then there are plenty of seminars that will not only break down the Franchise Disclosure Document for you, but will also show you how to finance your purchase and how and what to negotiate to get the best deal to fit your market and circumstances. Some of the topics you may be interested in include "Navigating the Buying Process: What to Ask Before You Invest," "Use Your IRA or 401(k) Money to Start a New Business," "The Franchisor-Franchisee Relationship: Striking the Perfect Balance," "Opportunities for Veterans in Franchising," and "Financing Options for Franchising: Your Best Alternatives Today," among several others available during the convention event.

If you are interested in franchising your business, then attending conferences specifically offered on topics concerning becoming a franchisor or becoming a better franchisor will certainly improve your chances at a profitable and harmonious relationship with your franchisees. Seminar topics available to you include "The Profitability of Franchising," "Operations Manuals: The Foundation to Consistent Execution," and "Best Practices for Start-up and Early-Stage Franchisors," along with other seminars dealing with brand consistency and other best practices.

Certified Franchise Executive Opportunities

After becoming a franchisee, and for those serious about franchising, they often enroll in the International Franchise

Association's Franchise University to become a Certified Franchise Executive (CFE) through its Institute of Certified Franchise Executives (ICFE). As a CFE, you have the opportunity to show everyone that you are passionate about the franchise industry and the expansion of your personal knowledge. Within the ICFE are opportunities to network with other individuals with similar drive, earn industry recognition for your achievements, and overall continue learning and growing professionally in the franchising community. But do not do this before becoming a franchisee, which would be putting the cart before the horse and thus a waste of your time at this point.

Overall, Why Should I Attend?

A better question to ask yourself might be, "Why am I not attending?" If you are looking for the opportunity to expand your knowledge of franchising, learn what it takes to be successful, earn credits toward your Certified Franchise Executive status, or simply find out if you have what it takes, the seminars offered at the franchise conventions will give you everything you need and more.

A prime example of why you should attend the seminars involves a young man who was interested in buying a personal services franchise. After attending our seminar "Navigating the Buying Process: What to Ask Before You Invest," this young man stated that prior to attending the seminar, he did not know that the Franchise Disclosure Document and franchise agreement could hold so many vague terms or that there was a possibility that he could negotiate the terms. After reading the FDD and attempting negotiations with the franchisor, he reported that he was successful in clarifying and negotiating many terms that mattered most to him and that without the different seminars that he had attended, he probably would have signed the franchise agreement as is, assuming that it was nonnegotiable or not tailorable to his circumstances and geographical issues, and cost himself thousands in possible revenues.

Many of the top-level franchising executives, speakers, and gurus volunteer their time every year to give back to the franchising community by providing sound advice and best practices to those wanting to break into franchising or improve their position within the franchise industry. With most of the speakers at the franchise shows having between five and 30 years' experience in franchising, you can rest assured that you are listening and conversing with professionals with the credentials to help you with whatever concerns you might have.

If franchising is right for you, it would behoove you to take advantage of these free and low-cost consultations in the various franchising niches.

"You have to learn to listen and listen to learn; because those that quit learning are dead." ~F. Gilson (author's great-grandmother)

CHAPTER 5

Working with Brokers, Consultants, and Salespeople

By Lynne Shelton

Talking with franchise brokers can help you learn about businesses that offer a franchise model. Many times, perspective franchisees report back that they would have never considered a particular business if they hadn't been shown it by their franchise broker. Keep in mind, though, that every franchise you consider should be finely tuned to your personality type.

Therefore, usually the first test that a franchise broker will give you is a personality type test. Next, the franchise brokers will do a review based on the amount of money you have to spend to perform the build-out or setup of the business. The next step they will usually take is to compare that to your personality type. For example, if you want to be a manager of several employees, then they will see what types of businesses are available that have or that need a lot of employees that fit within your financial budget. Or if you are better on your own or with only one or two people under you, oftentimes franchise brokers will look for what type of home-based business would fit within your budget.

Once they have this information, they will likely present you with three different franchise systems for your review. Don't be surprised if they are within an industry that you've never even thought about working in or didn't even know that there were franchises in those industries. The important part at this stage is to keep an open mind to those industries. Your personality type is a huge factor in determining which one could be the best option for you. However, the one thing you want to avoid under most circumstances is a franchise that deals with your hobby. A hobby is defined as a pastime, a relaxing diversion, a fad, or an interest. If you want to keep it that way, don't combine your hobby with your business because it will now be work for you, not fun time, as a hobby should be.

Remember that a franchise consultant or broker is a salesperson, meaning that they can only sell you from the inventory that they have in stock. To obtain the most options that fit with your personality type and your financial abilities, you should engage with more than one franchise consultant or franchise broker so that you can look at as many franchises that fit you as possible. Never sign an exclusive sales agreement with a franchise consultant or a franchise broker. This will stop you from being able to shop around.

CHAPTER 6

Risk of Investment and How to Mitigate Risk

By Lynne Shelton

Everyone wants to mitigate their business risk, but how do you do that in reality?

In this chapter, we want to go over some of the more common risks that can be associated with franchise systems. We will use Joe as our example.

When Joe retired, he decided to buy a popular fast-food franchise. The salesperson assured Joe that he would soon be making lots of money. But almost a year after signing his franchise agreement, Joe still doesn't have a location for his restaurant. Each time Joe found a location he liked, the franchisor rejected his choice. Frustrated, Joe went back over papers he got before he bought his franchise. Joe noticed that more than half of all franchisees in his system failed to open in their first year, and many never opened at all. Joe also saw that the franchisor could terminate his franchise—and keep his $30,000 franchise fee—if he doesn't open his restaurant at an approved location within 12 months.

Some people believe that owning a franchise is a safe and easy way to start a successful business. But as Joe—and many others like Joe—learned, buying a franchise can be risky, and there is no guarantee of success, especially in an uncertain economy. If you are thinking about investing in a franchise, you must educate yourself before you buy, which is why it is so important to not only read the franchise agreement but to do the due diligence prior to signing it by hiring professionals to help you evaluate the risks associated with that particular franchise system. Below is a discussion of 15 of the most common risks that should be reviewed with your franchise attorney prior to signing a franchise agreement, so you don't end up like Joe.

15 Considerations Before Investing in a Franchise

1. **Renewal conditions.** Most franchise agreements are limited to a specific term, usually five, 10, or 20 years. You may not have an automatic right to renew. Even if you can renew, you may have to satisfy certain conditions, like signing a new agreement with entirely different terms and higher fees, or face losing your business. You will find this information in the FDD in Item 17.

2. **Legal counsel.** Franchise agreements are drafted by the franchisor's attorney. They almost always give the franchisor every advantage. If you do not use a franchise attorney to advise and assist you before you invest, you place yourself at a serious disadvantage.

3. **Get it in writing.** Franchisor salespersons and franchise brokers don't represent your interests. They may promise you many things about a franchise before you buy, but if that promise is not stated in writing in your franchise agreement, it is unenforceable and means nothing.

4. **No easy way out.** You may not have an easy way to close your franchise business, even if it fails. Some franchisors can actually sue for expected "future royalties" if you terminate your franchise agreement early. Additionally, there may be additional liquidated damages if you intentionally do something to harm the franchise system or the brand as a whole. What you have to do to terminate is covered in Item 17.
5. **Franchisor control.** Most franchise agreements require you to accept the franchisor's system changes, such as menu items, advertising, or a whole new decor, no matter how costly or unwise you consider them to be. You may be able to negotiate in advance with your franchise attorney's assistance a reasonable cap on those expenses. These requirements are shown in Items 8, 11, 15, 16, and 17 of the FDD.
6. **Dispute resolution.** Many franchise agreements allow for the resolution of disputes in the state where the franchisor's headquarters is located. It may be expensive and inconvenient for you to travel to assert your rights, even if your claims are valid. Franchisors often require that disputes be "arbitrated," which can further limit your rights and remedies. We would recommend that you change this to mediation instead of arbitration, which is much more beneficial to the franchisee and is almost always a less expensive option. Additionally, many states' laws require the mediation to be in the franchisee's home state, which is an additional cost savings. This is discussed in Item 17 of the FDD.

7. **Designated suppliers.** Most franchise agreements require that you buy goods or services from suppliers the franchisor designates or approves. You may not be getting the best deal for these goods and services because the supplier may be affiliated with the franchisor or may pay the franchisor a rebate based on your purchases. We recommend adding a safeguard clause that allows you to purchase products from a supplier of your choosing if it meets "brand standards" and is cheaper than the cost of the approved supplier. This information is disclosed in Item 8 and 16 in the FDD.
8. **Restrictions on method of operation.** Franchisors mostly require that you operate in a particular way; for instance, they may dictate the hours of operation and preapprove your signage, the employee uniforms, and all forms of advertisements. They can also mandate which accounting system, Point-of-Service software, and bookkeeping procedures you use. Some franchise agreements also require you to sell certain products or services at designated national pricing and restrict the number of discounts or markups that you can do. If your franchise agreement has these provisions in them, it is imperative that you negotiate these items in advance of signing the agreement or you will be locked into those terms for the full Term of the Agreement, whether it be five years or 20 years. This is disclosed in Items 8, 15, and 16 of the FDD.
9. **Territory and sales area.** There are two types of territories: an Exclusive Territory and a Nonexclusive Territory. An Exclusive Territory provides protection from the franchisor selling additional franchisees within the territory given to

you, and it also precludes the franchisor from placing a corporate location in your territory. While territorial restriction may ensure that you will not compete with other franchisees for the same customers, they also could hurt your ability to open additional outlets or to move to a more profitable location without advanced permission. You must also pay particular attention to the internet side of sales. A franchisor may limit your ability to have a website or to sell products and services online. Additionally, some franchisors give themselves the right to offer goods or services in your sales area through its own website or through catalogs or telemarketing campaigns. The territory type that will be granted will be disclosed in Item 12 of the FDD.

10. **Termination.** You can lose your right to your franchised business if you breach the franchise agreement. The franchise agreement is for a limited time, and your right to renew is not a forgone conclusion; it is usually not guaranteed, although some states require it if you are in good standing with the franchisor. A franchisor can terminate your franchise agreement for a variety of reasons, including your failure to pay royalties or abide by the performance standards and sales restrictions in the agreement. You can see a list of all the items that can be terminated for by looking in the FDD in Item 17 under the subsection "Cause defined." You will lose your investment if your franchise agreement is terminated, and you may owe the liquidated damages and other expenses mentioned above as well.

11. **Renewal and transfers.** The term of a franchise agreement can vary from a typical five-year to a 20-year term, although the most common term is 10 years. You should take into consideration FranklinCovey's famous habit, "begin with the end in mind," meaning that before you begin working in the franchise relationship, you should plan on how you would like to choose to end the relationship. We always ask potential franchisees what their exit strategy is, meaning when you are done being a franchisee or working in the business, how do you want to get out? Usually, people will fall into one of three categories: they either want to 1) give it to their kids or other family members, 2) continue working in the business until they die (they don't plan on retiring ever), or 3) they want to sell it off and go lay on a beach (or whatever your idea of bliss is). These items usually should have some form of negotiation or amendments to the franchise agreement completed by your franchise attorney. Most franchise agreements do not allow you to pick two of the three of those items as the agreement is written. You must negotiate for those rights in advance of signing the agreement. For renewals, some franchise systems do not give you the right of renewal, or they may place additional requirements that you must have done or not done in order to be eligible for renewal in the system. You can see these items also in Item 17 of the FDD. Even if you have the right to renew, it may not be at the same terms you had during your initial franchise agreement terms or conditions. In fact, the franchisor may have the right to raise the royalty payments, impose a new design

standard or new sales restrictions, or reduce your territory. Any changes that occur may result in more competition from company-owned outlets or other franchisees as well.

12. **Contact franchisees.** Every franchisee must receive a Franchise Disclosure Document at least 14 days before investing. The FDD contains important information about the franchise, including contact information for current and terminated franchisees. You should contact as many of these individuals as you can before you invest. Determine if a high number of franchisees have closed, transferred, or never opened. If experienced franchisees are not happy (or you cannot reach them), be very skeptical. Item 20 requires franchisors to disclose at least the closest 100 franchisees to your location. Because this is difficult to keep track of for most brands, they typically will just put all franchisees listed by state in the FDD so you can locate the closest ones to you. However, because that list can grow quite large, most FDDs have this list in an exhibit attached to the FDD, so the location of it will vary from franchisor to franchisor, but you can locate it by looking at the Table of Contents within the first few pages of the FDD. The list of franchisees must contain three components to be legally binding: a) the list of active franchisees or area developers that are open for business, b) franchisees and area developers that have signed the agreement with the franchisor but are not yet open for business, and c) a list of franchisees that they have lost contact with for 10 months or more, plus terminated or nonrenewed franchisees. Make sure you contact some of the franchisees from all three sections of this list. For a

white paper on what questions to ask, see the Articles section on the Shelton Law website (www.SLA.Law/Articles).

13. **Financial representation disclosures.** Most franchisors choose not to disclose earnings of existing franchisees in their FDD, even though this disclosure is allowed. There may be several reasons why a franchisor would not disclose this information, but one reason may be that its franchisees are not profitable, or maybe they don't require their franchisees to report this information to the franchisor in the franchise agreement. You can see if the franchise system you are looking at provides them by looking at Item 19 of the FDD. All locations that have been open for one year or more must be included if they disclose any information. Cherry-picking the best locations' numbers only is no longer legally allowed.

14. **Background check.** Fifteen states have laws that regulate the sale of franchises. In those states, the franchisor must be preregistered. You can see where a franchisor is registered by looking at the table, which could be in one of two places in your FDD depending on where you live. It could be at the front of the FDD within the first few pages, or it could be at the end of the FDD right in front of the Receipt pages you were asked to sign saying that you received the FDD on a specific date. It is a good idea to contact the state attorney general's office to find out if the franchisor is registered and if it has received any complaints by franchisees.

15. **Personnel.** Businesses in the same industry or vertical can be run very differently. One of the items you should consider about a particular franchise system is their personnel requirements. Can it or must it be owner-operated, meaning that you have to work full-time in the business. If it does not have to be owner-operated, are you required to hire a manager that will be responsible for the day-to-day running of the business? If you do have to hire a manager, must they attend training? And if they do have to attend training, how long prior to opening the business must training occur? This will tell you when you must hire a manager by. It is common to have a franchisee have a manager on payroll for several months prior to actually opening the business to the public, which of course costs additional funds than a franchise where you are not required to hire a manager and send them to training. Additionally, if the manager must attend the franchisor's training, must every manager attend franchisor's training? If so, every time a manager quits, you will have to hire another manager and send them to training before you can use them for staffing. Not only can this get costly if you are not good at hiring the right person, but it will leave you working in your business until the manager is trained each time. The personnel requirements should be shown and listed out in Item 8 and Item 11 of the FDD. They could also be negotiated by your franchise attorney to change the requirements to "may" clauses: "you *may* send your managers to franchisor's training," etc. You will find this information in Item 15 of the FDD.

Additional Resources — Consumer Protection

Besides the suggestions contained in this book, several other resources can help with franchisee's protection within the franchise setting.

Oversight of franchise and business opportunity offerings is an important consumer protection for hundreds of thousands of people who invest in these operations. It requires careful attention by both federal and state authorities.

At the state level, oversight of franchising is grounded in the traditional commitment of grassroots officials to protect consumers whenever possible before they part with their money and, in those cases where money is lost in a fraudulent deal, to marshal the enforcement resources to shut down the violator and seek restitution if possible.

California adopted the first state franchise statute in 1971. Today, several states, including Hawaii, Illinois, Indiana, New York, Virginia, Washington, North and South Dakota, Maryland, Michigan, Minnesota, Rhode Island, and Wisconsin, have statutes that regulate the offering of franchises for sale. These statutes are designed to provide greater protections to prospective franchisees and prevent fraud in the sale of franchise offerings.

You can find information about state franchising offices at the following website: www.nasaa.org/Industry-Resources/Franchise-Resources/.

CHAPTER 7

Negotiating a Franchise Agreement from the Franchisee's and Franchisor's Perspective

By Lynne Shelton

Let's explore negotiating a franchise agreement using an example: The franchisee wants a two-mile radius instead of the standard one-mile radius the FDD states.

Franchisor's Perspective

A general rule, as stated before, is that franchisors do not want to set a trend for future franchise buyers by negotiating dollars and percentages. This is because if a franchisor discounts a royalty fee, marketing fee, or the initial franchise fee, then they have to disclose that negotiation in the FDD or through special filings with the state attorney general's office for future franchise buyers to see. This creates the trend that future franchise buyers want to get the same deal that the other buyer received, which has led many franchisors to have a take-it-or-leave-it mentality.

If you are interested in having a larger territory, then think about the give-and-take that you can work with to acquire the larger territory, which does not always mean paying twice the franchise fee for twice the territory. Everyone wants to pay lower fees, but that is not going to happen for most franchise systems, but it is possible to get something more valuable to you, and the franchisor, like territory.

Franchisors want to deal with the least amount of people possible, thus saving in support costs. An Area Development Agreement (ADA) is a multiunit agreement over time. By selling you an ADA, they get to show more units sold in the FDD. Due to the growth it shows in the FDD, it helps them to sell more franchises, so franchisors often give a 10% to 50% discount on ADAs for the franchisee's requirement to open within a predetermined development schedule. Thus, the franchisor agrees that you can have two miles if you agree to open two stores over a predetermined amount of time.

Franchisee's Perspective

The franchisee wants a two-mile radius because a new shopping center has been approved to be built within two years. The FDD says the franchisee can market into territories not developed with no penalty. The ADA shows 50% off all units over one. If the franchisee buys two territories, it will cost the same as one unit.

Development schedule: Negotiate to at least a five-year development time for unit #2. When the shopping center opens, you, as the franchisee, will have up to three more years before having to pay for and develop the second location.

Negotiating Your Next Deal in Advance

If you know that you want or need to make modifications or additions to your relationship with the franchisor in the future, it is best to do so up front.

First, let's discuss our example for this chapter—the shopping center being built in two years. Let's say you also have a nephew who is business savvy and in his last two years of his master's degree program, and he wants to potentially run the second location once you develop it. However, it is common for franchisors to restrict any transfers or change of ownership in the franchisee company. A common provision in the franchise agreement will state something like:

"The rights and duties of Franchisee as set forth in this Agreement, and the franchise herein granted, are personal to Franchisee (or its owners), and Franchisor has entered into this Agreement in reliance upon Franchisee's (or its owners') personal or collective skills and financial ability. Accordingly, except for percentage of ownership transfers inter se, neither Franchisee nor any holder of a legal or beneficial interest in Franchisee may sell, assign, convey, give away, pledge, mortgage, sublicense or otherwise transfer, whether by operation of law or otherwise, any interest in this Agreement."

This means that unless you negotiate in advance to allow your nephew to become an owner or predetermined approved manager for the second location, you might be stuck with paying a transfer fee or, worse yet, a flat-out denial of your plan.

Oftentimes we hear that there doesn't need to be an amendment to the franchise agreement, but that "it's okay, we have spoken to the franchisor, and they are fine with X [whatever you are negotiating[when it comes to that point in time." That is a very risky place to leave decisions. The current franchisor may be a person of his or her word; however, there is no guarantee that who the franchisor is today will be the same people when "that point in time" arrives. More and more venture capital firms are buying franchise systems. In fact, the number of franchise brands acquired by private equity firms rose from *24* in 2012 to *60* in 2018; in six short years, it almost tripled. There have been many horror stories about private equity or venture capital firms buying franchise systems and changing the entire culture of the system.

The private equity investor may want to sell the system or certain of its assets quickly, require the franchisees to make capital expenditures to acquire new equipment, update the entire look of the location (remember Wendy's and KFC's rebranding) or offer new services, or embark on a program to "clean house" by more robustly enforcing standards and terminating nonperforming franchisees.

This is just a good reminder to "get it in writing" any of the "promises" that are being told to you by the franchisor or their salesperson. If you get it in writing, then the future will not hold any potential booby traps for you, and you can go forward in confidence that your wishes will be fulfilled by the franchisor. Now you can just focus on following the system.

CHAPTER 8

Franchisor Days

By Lynne Shelton

You will want to attend any of several franchisor-sponsored events or days if they are offered in the franchise system you are evaluating.

Discovery Days

Companies schedule Discovery Days in different ways: once a month, once a quarter, or anytime a candidate can make it! As the franchise system grows, the franchisor will be forced to schedule more frequent and specific dates so they don't overtax their home office resources.

But for you, attending a Discovery Day should be looked at as something that is done sooner better than later. Like a cold steak, your opportunity can lose its sizzle the longer the wait for Discovery Day. Unexpected events in your world may postpone or kill the event entirely. Discovery Day is showtime, so the better prepared you and your family are, the more successful the trip will be. Get affirmation from the franchisor that they are ready for you to join the franchise system, if you accept them, barring any unforeseen circumstances.

Franchise consultants always coach their candidates to present themselves professionally to help ensure review committee approval;

that is good advice for you to remember. It's time for both of you to meet, get to know each other, and confirm this is a good match. Be sure to put your best foot forward! It is important for their staff to know who you are and believe that you can be successful in their business. Express yourselves. Show your personality and interest in the franchise program. Prepare at least two questions to ask at your meetings with operations, real estate, and our senior executive staff. Prospective buyers should also be ready to answer questions for executive committee approval, such as, "Why do you feel we should award this opportunity to you?" and "What contributions do you believe you can bring to our system?" Some franchisors have the president or CEO conduct a pre-Discovery Day interview with a candidate before they are approved to attend. This interim step further qualifies the buyer's interest, expectations, and suitability before both parties invest their time and expense in the Discovery Day event.

Your candidate personality profiles should be completed at least a week prior to the Discovery Day and forwarded, along with your applications and other relevant information, to the franchisor's executive review committee. Committee members will reference these files when considering whether to give you their franchise approval before, during, or immediately after Discovery Day. Mobile Bankers, a mobile check-cashing franchise, thoroughly qualifies candidates for Discovery Day. The franchisor reported that they required each candidate to prepare a preliminary business plan (less any financial projections) for presentation to their review committee. Potential franchisees were instructed to 1) express their ideas on how they would set up their business, 2) present local marketing ideas to build customers, and 3) share how they saw their role in the business initially and long-term. This type of interactive assignment further engages you in the business, demonstrates your skill sets, and provides a snapshot of how prepared you are for the franchise. You need to be prepared to be fully vetted and evaluated by the franchisor while you are completing your due diligence on them.

Join the Team Day

Not every company offers a Join the Team Day, but those that do make it a staple in their sales process. A Join the Team Day is a crescendo to the due diligence and sales process of you buying the franchise. It is the event both parties have been waiting for. It is the time and location where you will get all last-minute questions answered and finish any due diligence requirements that the franchisor has. After both parties have finished their due diligence, it is then time to sign the franchise agreement with the franchisor.

SECTION III

AFTER YOU JOIN YOUR CHOSEN FRANCHISE SYSTEM

CHAPTER 9

Maximizing Brand Value for Everyone's Benefit

By Lynne Shelton

Brand Value

Likely the franchisor worked for many years to avoid doing all the wrong things. They have focused on growing their brand value. The recognition of a brand as a valuable asset is relatively recent. Back in the 1950s, business success and consumer choice were "defined solely on product quality and value, not the name on the tin," according to *The Atlantic*. They also stated, "The advertising boom of the 1960s turned company identities into household names, bringing them into public consciousness through the medium of marketing. Brand names became a proxy for desirable characteristics like sleek design, durability, refinement, service, and innovation."

Nowadays, it's hard to imagine making purchase decisions without brand coming into play, so immersed are we in the culture of brand identity and meaning as well as what other consumers think of that brand. The App Store and Google Play are littered with applications that can show you the opinions of others. Webpages on most of the larger resellers have ratings and rankings on how this particular product or service has been reviewed by others. Does it have a 4.5 out of 5.0 rating? Or maybe it has 4 stars listed by the business.

We instinctively look to the brand name of an item to help determine its value. Little wonder, then, that today's brands are valuable commodities that are built, nurtured, and even bought and sold between companies. Brand value is the monetary worth of your brand if you were to sell it.

If your company were to merge or be bought out by another business, and they wanted to use your name, logo, and brand identity to sell products or services, your brand value would be the amount they would pay you for that right. This is known as market-based **brand value**.

Another way to think of brand value is in terms of replacement cost (cost-based brand value). In this sense, brand value is the amount you would need to spend to design, execute, promote, and amplify a totally new brand to the same level as your old one. That figure might include the cost of hiring a design agency, the time and effort spent on marketing and social media strategy, the cost of advertising, PR outreach and sponsorship, and so on.

For franchise systems and businesses alike, brand value comes from its intellectual property. There are four intellectual property rights: patent, copyright, trademark, and trade secrets.

A **patent** is the exclusive right to the benefits of an invention or improvement right that is issued by the government agency, the United States Patent and Trademark Office (commonly referred to as USPTO), for a specific period of time on the basis that it is novel (not previously known or described in a publication). An example of a patent is the ornamental design for the 2021-filed Coca-Cola bottle design, shown here as listed at the USPTO. Patents have very specific claims that are included in their protection, which they can exclude others from using.

Bottle

DOCUMENT ID	DATE PUBLISHED		
US D959273 S	2022-08-02		

INVENTOR INFORMATION

NAME	CITY	STATE	ZIP CODE
Joshi, Rohit	Alpharetta	GA	N/A
Bleakney, Abagail	Atlanta	GA	N/A
Safiullah, Mohammad Adom	Diamond Bar	CA	N/A
Hossain, Naser	Diamond Bar	CA	N/A
Takaddus, Ahmed Tasnub	Diamond Bar	CA	N/A
Hanan, Jay	Diamond Bar	CA	N/A
Lai, Katherine	Diamond Bar	CA	N/A

APPLICANT INFORMATION

NAME	CITY	STATE	ZIP CODE
The Coca-Cola Company	Atlanta	GA	N/A

AUTHORITY	TYPE
N/A	assignee

ASSIGNEE INFORMATION

NAME	CITY	STATE	ZIP CODE
The Coca-Cola Company	Atlanta	GA	N/A

TYPE CODE			
02			

APPLICATION NO	DATE FILED
D/765068	2021-01-05

A **copyright** is the exclusive right of the author or creator of a literary or artistic property (such as a book, movie, or musical composition) to print, copy, sell, license, distribute, transform to another medium, translate, record, or perform or otherwise use (or not use) and to give it to another by will. One example of a copyright, shown below, would be *The lion, the witch and the wardrobe*© by C. S. Lewis for its dramatization completed by Don Quinn. Copyrights are registered at the United States Copyright Office now. Until recently, they were registered through the Library of Congress.

Below is an excerpt of what a registered copyright looks like when searching at the U.S. Copyright Office. The italicized verbiage at the top is the name of the copyright as it is registered.

The lion, the witch and the wardrobe. C. S. Lewis, dramatization by Don...

Type of Work: Dramatic Work and Music; or Choreography
Registration Number / Date: RE0000739761 / 1996-12-09
Renewal registration for: DP0000006648 / 1968-03-18
Title: The lion, the witch and the wardrobe. C. S. Lewis, dramatization by Don Quinn.
Copyright Claimant: Don Quinn (A)
Basis of Claim: New Matter: dramatization.
Variant title: The lion, the witch and the wardrobe
Names: Lewis, C. S.
Quinn, Don

A **trademark** is a distinctive design, picture, emblem, logo, or wording (or combination) affixed to goods for sale to identify the manufacturer as the source of the product. Words that merely name the maker (but without particular lettering) or a generic name for the product are not trademarks. Trademarks may be registered with the USPTO to prove use and ownership. Use of another's trademark (or one that is confusingly similar) is infringement and the basis for a lawsuit for damages for unfair competition and/or a petition for an injunction (a court order) against the use of the infringing trademark). An example of a well-recognized trademark is Nike's swish, both in black and in white appearance, and, of course, just the name NIKE, as shown below.

Typed Drawing
74612654

NIKE

And last, a **trade secret** is a process, method, plan, formula, or other information unique to a manufacturer that gives it an advantage over competitors. Therefore, the trade secret has value and may be protected by a court-ordered injunction against use or revelation of trade secrets by an employee, former employee, or someone else who comes into possession of the trade secret. One of the most recognized trade secrets would be KFC®'s secret herbs and spices on their chicken or the recipe for Coca-Cola® original, now known as Coca-Cola Classic®.

A great example of how large your intellectual property portfolio can grow over time is with Coca-Cola Company, Inc. Taking a look at their Balance Sheet, which can be found on their Investors page of their website at https://investors.coca-colacompany.com/financial-information, it shows as of the summer of 2022, that Coca-Cola's Brand Value totaled more than the amount of its physical Total Current Assets **(bolded)**. Let's break this down by looking at the Current Assets portion of that Balance Sheet.

CONDENSED CONSOLIDATED BALANCE SHEETS — USD ($)
$ in Millions Jul. 01, 2022

CURRENT ASSETS

Cash and cash equivalents	$8,976
Short-term investments	776
Total Cash, Cash Equivalents and Short-Term Investments	9,752
Marketable securities	1,867
Trade accounts receivable, less allowances of $510 and $516, respectively	4,494
Inventories	3,621
Prepaid expenses and other current assets	3,407
TOTAL CURRENT ASSETS	**23,141**
Equity method investments	17,720
Other investments	655
Other noncurrent assets	6,470
Deferred income tax assets	1,833
Property, plant and equipment, less accumulated depreciation of $9,099 and $8,942, respectively	9,462
TRADEMARKS WITH INDEFINITE LIVES	**14,271**
GOODWILL	**18,910**
OTHER INTANGIBLE ASSETS	**707**

The total amount of Brand Value is obtained financially by adding together the Trademarks with indefinite lives value + the Goodwill value + the Other intangible assets **(all bolded)**, which totals $33,888 (in millions), or written out for illustration, $33,888,000,000.00, in value. This is over $10 billion more than the amount of their physical assets! As demonstrated, brand value is extremely important to a business. This is the reason why franchise law and the court system take seriously the protection of a franchisor's brand and image from would-be infringers and defaulting franchisees.

Brand Equity

Whereas brand value is a financial gauge of your brand's worth, **brand equity** has to do with customer perceptions and how positive they are. Customers who prefer your brand to others and exhibit loyalty to your brand over time are contributing to your brand equity.

Brand Value vs. Brand Equity

Brand equity can be viewed as a factor influencing brand value, since in building your brand equity, you're contributing to the qualities that will make it valuable—things like brand recognition, positive associations with quality and service, and aspirational value. All these factors promote revenue by driving customer spending and customer loyalty.

Using Psychographics to Calculate Brand Equity

Today data compiling and tracking of customers has become second nature in the business world. Whether companies are using the old-fashioned United States Census data and internet searches or the more commonplace social media and GPS (global positioning system) data, we are being tracked: our every move, our comings and goings, what we like, buy, ask about, or research. That is where the ever-powerful psychographics come into play. Psychographics is a qualitative methodology used to describe traits of humans using psychological attributes. Psychographics have been applied to the study of personality, values, opinions, attitudes, interests, and lifestyles.

Many companies specialize in psychographics, ranging from SaaS (software as a service) providers such as Placer.ai, who claim to provide "unprecedented visibility into consumer foot-traffic," to psychographic data compilers such as MRI-Simmons, who "employs probabilistic and address-based sampling, widely considered to be the gold standard methodology by marketers and researchers alike." They utilize partners and companies such as Equifax, esri, Acxiom, and Nielsen to keep a pulse on American consumers.

But is this important to franchising? Extremely so! Let's use an example: Say that you are trying to figure out if you should buy a particular specialty drink franchised business that is in operation. You know that you live in a metropolitan city and would like to have the business in your city, but you don't care where exactly it is, you just want it to be profitable. This is an often-repeated wish of franchisees we speak to. At Shelton Law & Associates, we recommend utilizing psychographics for all our franchisors so that they have a built-in real estate program for their franchisees. When we run the psychographics report for a particular brand, it shows us not only where the buyers are (for marketing purposes), but also the brand equity for any particular location that you are evaluating whether to purchase resale. Individuals becoming franchisees should utilize this same powerful data to ensure a successful location. Let's walk through an example. Not wanting to give away our particular client's data, let's use a national average in this example and say that this business will use 300 customer servings a day (the average of the usual 100–500 servings/customers a day). We look at the underlying data and see that there is a brand loyalty of 23% of customers that repeat their visits to the business at least four times per month. Thus, if we use 30 days in a month, then there are an approximate 9,000 customers per month when multiplied by the brand loyalty percentage (23%); we can determine that 2,070 repeat customers come to the location at least four times to order product. If the average customer ticket price is $16.00, then we can easily calculate the brand equity in this case: 2,070 x $16.00 equals $33,120. That is over $33,000 of brand equity that you could count on repeating every month if you bought that location. Additionally, if we, for sake of ease, say the remaining 77% of the customers (6,930) all only came once per month, we can figure that we will earn an approximate $110,880 per month from them as well. So, this location builds approximately $144,000 in brand equity each month.

One could also utilize psychographics to determine whether a business would be successful in a particular location. Looking at where the customers live and work and where they frequent can give insight as to whether there would be enough customers to sustain another location in close proximity or within a specific area, neighborhood, or community. Additionally, psychographics can also tell whether a new location would cannibalize customers from an existing location. Psychographics can be used for so many business decisions, this example only scratches the surface of how they can be used.

Brand Value without Brand Equity?

However, a brand can also have value without having equity. For example, in the pre-release phase of a product, a company would spend money and invest value into developing a brand before its future customers ever see it. Brand equity is linked to both reputation and brand purpose, since these relate to how a customer's personal values align to a brand, and the resulting bond that forms between them.

Compared with brand value, brand equity is a more nebulous concept and harder to measure, since it relates to consumer motivation, opinion, and behavior rather than financial figures.

How to Measure Brand Value

Today's appreciation of the power of brands means there is a wide array of viewpoints on what makes a brand successful, how brands interact with consumer psychology, and even what the true definition of brand should be. Predictably, measuring brand value can be difficult and baffling without a clear approach in mind.

That said, the most fundamental ways of measuring brand value are still quite simple. One of the most straightforward methods is to ask other companies what they would pay for the rights to your brand. This is what franchisors do for their brands. They have asked the experts in franchising for an honest evaluation of what their brand is worth to a franchisee to become part of the system. This amount turns into the "Initial Fees" that are reflected in Item 5 of the Franchise Disclosure Document.

When it comes time to sell your franchised location, you will also be looking to the brand value to assist you in earning your return on profit from building up your brand equity and location. Although this number changes over the years, most currently, the average is around three to five times EBITDA based on your current annual gross sales. **EBITDA** is short for earnings before interest, taxes, depreciation, and amortization. It is one of the most widely used measures of a company's financial performance, financial health, and ability to generate cash.

By doing this calculation, you'd get a range of figures you could average out to arrive at a fair market value for your franchise location. Using the previous example for the brand equity that showed psychographics proving $144,000 per month, when multiplied by 12 months in a year, that equals $1,728,000 per year. If we use 3x EBITDA, that would be approximately $5,184,000.00, ranging up to 5x EBITDA, which gives a value of $8,640,000.00 that your location should resell for.

Nonfranchised businesses range around one to two times EBITDA, although that can certainly change depending on what the business is and the demand for that particular company.

The other way you can measure brand value is to gather quotes from providers or make internal projections to find out how much it would cost to develop a brand equivalent to your current one. In other words, go back to the beginning and attempt to figure out how much it would cost to do it all over again. As this method does not rely on solid financial figures, the margin for error with this valuation method is larger.

The Brand Value Chain

An important milestone in the development of brand-building strategy is the **brand value chain model**. This is a four-step schematic developed by marketing experts Keller and Lehman in 2003. It describes how brand value can be built through marketing and the impacting factors that affect progress along the path of growth.

As it was developed in 2003, the brand value chain does not specifically take into account digital marketing and how brand value and reputation are built online and, in particular, how digital culture has changed consumer behavior. However, it can provide a useful framework for building and quantifying brand value.

Building Your Brand Value

Here are a few of the ways you can enhance your brand's equity and, ultimately, your brand value:

1. Marketing and Advertising

Marketing helps you to move from brand awareness and recognition to understanding, alignment, and loyalty from your customers.

According to the original definition, brand value chains start with marketing as the first step to realizing brand value since it establishes the brand in the mind of the customer.

2. Ambassadorship and Sponsoring

Whether it's sports stars, social media influencers, or musicians, aligning with a well-known individual or group is a well-established norm of brand building. It not only raises awareness and recognition of your brand, but it can also be linked with brand purpose, where your company's ethical and social values are enhanced and amplified by your choice of ambassador. Choose wisely!

3. Customer Experience

Providing great customer experience is a powerful way to boost brand equity. As much as quality products and services, customers increasingly expect a good experience from brands, and research has shown that many are willing to pay more and choose brands ahead of their competitors when they've enjoyed a positive experience.

In summary, building brand value and brand equity are important parts of any business. Marketing, sponsorship, and customer experience play a large roll in what will become your business value.

Resources Smart Owners Use to Build Their Businesses

The next tool to consider in building your business is your available resources. Today business owners, corporations, and associations are faced with financial restrictions, new state and federal requirements, and employee standards. These changes are leaving many business owners anxious and questioning their business practices.

Even the most well-established companies and those considering starting a business or purchasing a franchise are exploring new resources and practices to endure these challenging times. Increasingly, business owners are seeking business consultants, peer review boards, and business coaches to shed new light on the challenges they face and to offer innovative, practical techniques and solutions to maintain viable and profitable companies.

Successful business owners are willing to:
- Take off the rose-colored glasses and see the company as it actually is.

- Recognize their role or lack of role in the present condition of the company.
- Recognize that they don't know everything, be open to candid feedback, and be willing to implement new techniques and ideas even if they are uncomfortable.
- Invest in ongoing professional training for themselves and their employees.

Smart business owners, who want honest—sometimes brutally candid—feedback on how to effectively run their businesses and address difficult issues, consider joining an executive peer board or securing the services of a business coach or business consultant. Let's dive deeper into these three tools.

Peer Review Boards

Peer review boards, also referred to as peer advisory boards and executive mastermind groups, typically consist of noncompetitive business owners/professionals who meet once a month for a three- to four-hour board meeting. Members briefly discuss current industry events and issues. Each member is given time to address personal and business issues they are facing. Members offer practical, affordable advice and support in a structured, facilitated forum.

Benefits include:
- Practical real-life advice from people who have walked in your shoes
- A regular sounding board and accountability
- Candid discussion with people not beholden to you

Business Coach

Business owners and business professionals rarely if ever receive enough candid feedback to remain accountable. Either feedback doesn't exist or they are told what they expect to hear instead of what they *need* to hear. Coaching is a proven, effective process that helps anyone who wants to move to the next level of success. Based on assessment, feedback, and ongoing support, this process revitalizes and reenergizes individuals.

Benefits include:
- Objective, reliable insights about personal and professional strengths and improvement opportunities
- Opportunity to adapt to new responsibilities, reduce destructive behaviors, enhance teamwork, and support organizational changes.

Business Consultant

The right business consultant with the right expertise can save you money and time in the long term by helping you streamline operations, cut costs, negotiate better deals with vendors, and improve company morale. Hiring a consultant is something you should consider if you are making a large purchase decision; creating buzz around a product release or other event; or even performing damage control around negative social media, an unfortunate mishap, or customer complaints. Keep in mind that hiring a consultant you like and trust can be a lengthy process, even if your need is immediate, because you must take the time to interview and vet candidates.

A consultant's rate typically works out to be more than you'd pay a permanent employee, but you don't incur payroll taxes and benefit costs or don't have to find work for the employee once the special project is completed.

Remember that hiring a consultant or coach and joining a peer group will not be a quick fix but rather a long-term investment in your business, professional, and personal development.

Assembling a Wisdom Advisory Circle Can Ease Your Mind

In addition to the formal franchised advisory or peer-to-peer boards, many business owners are choosing to form their own "wisdom adviser circles" composed of seasoned professionals from all facets of business (marketing, finance, technology, business owners, etc.) whom they personally know and respect.

Format and benefits of advisory boards and circles should include:
- In-person confidential meetings that are regularly scheduled, with supportive phone contact as needed
- Practical business techniques from business experts who have walked in your shoes
- Minimization of critical mistakes
- Candid interactive discussion with experts and other business owners and professionals
- Discovery of how to adapt to new responsibilities, reduce destructive behaviors, improve retention, enhance teamwork, and support organizational changes

- The ability to serve as a confidential sounding board and offer immediate advice related to important decisions
- Access to the expertise and years of experience of the experts you selected

Developing Your Wisdom Advisory Circle

Be selective. Recruit individuals you can trust with detailed confidential company information, finances, etc., if you desire to truly benefit from their advice. First, list your areas of vulnerability or lack of knowledge and identify experts in your area that can address these needed areas.

Have it in writing. Put the advisers' position descriptions and limitations in writing. Make it clear that business decisions are ultimately yours and that the advisers are not liable for their advice.

Ask for extended commitment. Ask for a yearly commitment with the option to mutually agree to renew. Select and renew wisely. Adding new blood with new ideas and energy can be beneficial, while maintaining a core group is important for stability.

Show appreciation. Showing your appreciation can include a list of your advisers and their companies on your company website, stipends, small shares of equity, appreciation dinners, or personally selected gifts.

Whether you decide to join a formal advisory board or form your own wisdom advisory circle, it will require you to admit what you don't know, take off the rose-colored glasses, accept candid feedback, and put in the time to take action; otherwise, your board is a waste of both your and the advisers' time.

CHAPTER 10

10 Ways to Capitalize on Annual Meetings

By Lynne Shelton

For the most part, the annual meeting put on by the franchisor is always a great weekend (or few days) filled with team building, learning, networking, and development, and if it is done right, you will still be talking about last year's event.

This chapter will attempt to answer two questions: 1) Why are franchise conventions so important to a franchise brand? and 2) What actually makes for a really great franchise convention?

The answer to the first point is a simple one. An annual franchise conference is the one occasion each year when the entire franchise network comes together. Yes, all good franchise brands will provide forums for their franchisees to interact online in some way, but there's no substitute for bringing people together face-to-face. A franchise convention is much more than an excuse for a party, though. It's an opportunity to motivate yourself, to grow and develop the brand, and really consolidate and strengthen the franchisor-franchisee relationship that is so key to successful franchise systems.

Franchise conventions, just like the brands hosting them, vary hugely in size and scale, from exotic beachfront locations and black-tie celebrations to modest conference centers and buffet lunches. The key needs and wants of franchisor and franchisees from the event are the same across that spectrum: Both want the event to add value for the brand and for the individual business owners who operate within the franchise system. They are so important to the brand and its internal and external growth, even franchise systems that are just starting out, with little or no budget, create a convention with a wow factor through careful advanced planning.

To answer the second question, here are 10 things franchisors should make mandatory during their attendance at their annual franchise convention or get-together.

1. Attendance

Many franchisors from successful brands will set expectations around franchisee attendance being mandatory at the convention from the outset, at the stage of discovery discussions with a potential franchisee. They will make it clear that attendance is expected and is not to be viewed as an optional event. These annual meetings have such an impact that some brands even have added penalty fees for those franchise locations that do not attend the annual convention. Some systems also have created ambassadors to help new franchisees see the benefits prior to ever attending their first one. If you are asked to be an ambassador after your first year, do it! It's a great way to develop further insight from within the franchise team; having franchisee advocates who can get a buzz going throughout the rest of the network and highlight the real tangible benefits they've gained through attending in previous years is a fun and exciting way to grow the synergy within the franchise system.

2. Location and Timing

When franchisees are spread across a large geographical area, choosing a location for the annual convention can prove to be a challenge. Time and travel are always reported barriers to attendance by franchisees. It will never be possible to keep everyone happy, but most systems rotate the location each year, as it's the easiest solution to keeping things even. We recommend that you write it on your calendar as soon as the dates are released, usually at least a year in advance, and then schedule around it for your work and personal schedule. Most franchisors will try to avoid the franchisees' busiest periods of the year. Since they usually change locations each year, it can be a great way to visit different places across the country. Most franchisees I know also use this time to add on a couple of days and make it a vacation for their family. A lot of franchise systems also welcome spouses and/or families to the usual awards banquet, so they can experience the wins, which will help them to understand the culture and goals of the brand too.

3. Clear Message and Theme

Every year, the convention program will have a clear and different convention theme. There will always be at least one thing the franchisors want the franchisees to take away from the event, if not many. Make sure that you pay attention to the promotional materials, team-building activities, keynote speakers, and workshop content to ensure that you are focused on the main ideas that are being conveyed. These are also the items that you should take to your team back at home working in the franchised business.

4. Create Fun and Memorable Moments

All work and no play are not the recipe for an engaging franchise life. Even within the more "serious" corporate brands, elements of fun such as team-building games and photo booths will be available to break the ice among team members who may not know one another well. These create great photo opportunities. These memorable moments will be the ones you take with you, that you share, and that you remember year after year.

5. Structure Your Program Carefully

It's important to make sure that you keep yourself balanced during the convention, whether it is an event that lasts just one day or several. Whether or not written in the schedule, make sure that you include sufficient breaks for rest between learning so that you remain energized and engaged throughout the event. Although it is likely that you want to check your emails and switch your phones on at times during the day, don't do it. Instead, ensure you have built in time for relaxation and general chatting and networking with other franchisees. This can be as important as time spent in the conference room.

6. Create Excitement

A franchise convention is the perfect opportunity to launch something new. Whether that be a new product or service, a new system to make franchisees' lives easier, or perhaps a rebrand, it's the ideal opportunity to engage everyone, provide any necessary face-to-face training, and get everyone on board. And as franchisees, it can be the key to successfully rolling out changes; ensure you understand all aspects of the change and obtain the information you need to get everyone back at the business enthused and on board. It is always fun to leave feeling that you are returning home with something that will have a practical and positive impact on your business.

7. Educate

For you to feel as if there's real tangible benefit for you and for your businesses in making the effort to attend the convention, there needs to be a significant element of learning during the event. No matter the size of your franchise network and the nature of your business, you will learn during the convention through expert speakers and trainers or hands-on practical workshops. Savvy franchisors will gain input far ahead of the event from the franchise network as to what they would like to see in terms of additional training and development at the event. If you are asked about this by your franchisor, make sure you take time to thoroughly think through what you need or what would best help your business and convey that to the franchisor to maximize the impact.

8. Get Involved

When gathering feedback following my own franchisee conventions, the replies always highlight the value that attendees have gained from hearing from other franchisees. Longer-standing members of the franchise team have a wealth of experience to share, and most are only too pleased (and flattered) to be invited to be part of a panel discussion or to take to the floor in some other way. If you are asked about this from your franchisor, make sure you think back about what you wish you had known when you started and attempt to share that content. Your real-life stories are far more relevant and inspirational than any motivational speaker.

9. Celebrate Achievements

Although some critics think the jury's out on franchise network awards, it has been reported that some franchisors favor them while others do not. In my own brand, we recognize long service and whole team achievements rather than hand out individual performance-related awards, but I see the merits of both approaches. No matter what your system does, I would recommend bringing your family or at least your spouse, if you have one, to this celebration event, as well as your managers and their spouses or families. It provides motivation and inspiration to other family members and your team members. It also creates great photo ops for local public relations and your own team building later back home.

10. Give Feedback

After the event, and as immediately as possible, ensure that you give feedback as an attendee. Which parts of the convention did you enjoy the most? Which speakers or workshops added most value to you and your business? What would you like to see from next year's event? All of this will help as your franchisor begins to plan what next year's annual convention will look like.

Doing it right, a franchise convention will have a huge impact on your franchise life and your business overall. Not only does it reignite your passion, but it can also significantly improve your bottom lines through streamlining processes and increasing productivity and profit. Ultimately, a great franchise convention is a reminder to yourself and your team that being part of your brand is really all about being part of a team.

CHAPTER 11

Smart Business Practice

By Richard Avdoian

Six Pillars for Business Success

Over the years, I have worked with business owners and franchisees who have struggled to effectively move their businesses forward and to the next level. We begin by completing an internal audit addressing the six pillars that are the keys to establishing a solid business foundation. Focusing on these areas collectively will provide a manageable foundation that will help a business owner make strides in increasing productivity and profitability.

Passion

Typically, every business owner, entrepreneur, and startup say passion was instrumental in starting their business. As the owner, you are responsible for defining and communicating your passion while being totally engaged to accomplish your goals. Otherwise, you cannot expect your employees to carry the torch. Maintaining a creative, energized workplace will generate excitement and result in the delivery of exceptional customer service.

People (Workforce)

Take the time to recruit the best candidates to fill the right seats rather than hiring when in a crisis. Having clearly defined job descriptions, realistic expectations, appropriate resources, and effective leadership will inspire others to thrive and work as an effective, cohesive team. Employees want to be winners, and they achieve goals when they are effectively led and feel valued.

Preparation

Investing in employees' personal and professional development will convey that you are as invested in your employees as you are in productivity and profitability. As a leader, it is your task to create a work environment that inspires, guides, and fuels the employees' motivation and professional development. This will ensure continuous excitement, empowerment, and commitment to being actively engaged in all facets of customer service.

Planning

Business owners who allocate time weekly to work *on* the business rather than *in* it are more likely to avoid exhausting their finances and resources. Having a current and five-year business plan, a clear vision and mission statement, defined processes, and best practice meetings will help employees stay on course and measure progress. Without a consistent, well-written, effective planning process, it is unreasonable to expect your business to achieve its full potential.

Performance

If business owners fail to establish and clearly articulate specific performance goals for which employees are accountable, they are simply hoping goals will be accomplished. It is your responsibility to routinely check, keep records, educate and inspire employees, and take corrective action as necessary to improve overall performance.

Perseverance

Business owners need to anticipate and prepare for setbacks, decreased production, and strained cash flow, then when necessary, bite the bullet and forge on. You can also count on employees making mistakes, losing focus, and maybe losing sight of the established goals. As the owner, you need to lead, projecting optimism, rallying the employees during turbulent times, and pushing past them.

The growth of any successful business does not happen by accident. Keeping your eyes open and monitoring these six pillars will help keep everyone energized and will take your business in the direction you desire.

Secrets to Franchisee's Success

Many studies have identified the secrets to business success and key leadership qualities. Based on my work with business owners in over 40 industries, here are a few qualities and best practices:

1. Embrace fear. Allow yourself to be visionary, innovative, and daring. Set yourself and your business apart from the masses, dance to a different drummer, and shake things up to help avoid mediocrity and the status quo. Being the black sheep in the herd can prove to be key to your success.
2. Be persistent, work hard, and stay focused. Remember that Rome was not built in a day, so be vigilant, take it slow, and never give up when you hit a snag or two. Failure is part of

learning, so when you hit snags, embrace them and learn from them.

3. Read, read, and read. Learning is a lifetime journey. Attending seminars and workshops, gaining knowledge, and acquiring new skills are crucial to survival in business.

4. Join professional associations, chambers of commerce, and civic organizations. Consider joining your local chamber of commerce or industry association. Subscribe to their journals and newsletters and attend and participate in various networking events. Consider participating in and supporting civic/charity events, volunteering, serving on a charity or professional board, and donating your services.

5. Self-talk is everything. Maintain a positive attitude. Think, "I can and will be successful," not "I will fail." Avoid negative individuals and environments. Stay focused and do not let opinions and judgment of others derail you, distract you, or drain your energy and enthusiasm.

6. Take the necessary time to determine, set, and implement goals, both personal and professional. Goal setting is pointless without a detailed implementation plan. Implement a well-written, detailed plan of action. Enough already: Stop thinking and rethinking about goals. Nothing will change if you never implement a plan of action. Take charge, face your apprehension and your fears, and dive in.

7. Take time to do your homework and research details. Seek out all the facts, ask questions, acknowledge what you know and understand and what you don't, and get input from experts within and outside your business. Mistakes made are merely opportunities to learn and challenge your creative abilities.

8. Network, interact, and communicate effectively. One person does not make a team. Identify, involve, and motivate others within and outside your business.

When it is all said and done, the key is really to be truthful and transparent and live with integrity. So, take ownership; otherwise, don't waste your time—none of the above will matter.

Stop Wasting Valuable Time and Energy

Alright already. I have heard it enough: Business owners complain that they can't effectively manage their time and that they feel helpless and frustrated. Well, let's call a spade a spade: It really isn't time you need to manage; you have to learn how to manage yourself—your energy, attention, and actions—throughout the workday.

Keeping in sync with your self-awareness is very important to effectively deal with the endless demands of your time. Being in tune with your body system and behavior, knowing your strengths, and setting limits are important indicators for effective use and management of time.

Here are a few ways you can minimize feeling under the gun to complete tasks, conserve energy, and effectively master your use of time:

1. Establish set opening and closing workday hours. Business owners need to clearly separate work and personal/family time. Let's face it: We never accomplish all that we want or need to accomplish. Too often, business owners extend work hours only to tax their bodies, which can lead to poor decision-making and errors. Setting start and ending times helps maintain good mental health.

2. Schedule routine morning and afternoon break times and lunchtime. It is never a good idea not to eat lunch or to eat while working. You may believe you are using the time wisely, but you are taxing your body and mind. You need to use these times to nourish and reenergize your body and relax your mind to prepare to address the remainder of the day's tasks, meetings, and challenges. Avoid scheduling business lunches. Be selfish: Use the time to eat something, relax, and take care of you. Take a walk to clear your mind.

3. Determine whether you are an a.m. or p.m. person when it comes to peak performance (more alert, energized, and productive). You need to recognize that there are daily, weekly, and monthly tasks you either thoroughly enjoy or dread. If you are like most, you put off the dreaded tasks until the end of the day—bad idea unless you are a p.m. person. You will always find the energy and time to rally to tackle the tasks you enjoy. On the other hand, tackling tasks you dread when you are less alert and energized can be extremely taxing and frustrating and increase the chances of making errors and poor decisions.

4. Let it go: You do not need to know how to handle every aspect of your business. Spending valuable time learning new social media tactics or computer systems can be extremely time-consuming and stressful. Instead, use the time for efficiently working *on* your business and leave working *in* the business to your staff or by outsourcing the tasks.

5. Take immediate charge and set your priorities as to what really needs to be addressed and when. We often first tackle

tasks and projects we like regardless of their importance. We need to avoid putting daunting, time-sensitive tasks and projects off until later, which may lead to frantically working extended hours.

So, remember: The more you overextend yourself with meetings, appointments, and an endless to-do list that doesn't have realistic deadline dates, the greater the chances that you will be overwhelmed, frazzled, and stressed, which leads to being increasingly less effective. So, plan your daily tasks and projects accordingly to be most productive.

Ask and You Shall Receive What Your Business Needs

Why is it that some franchisees thrive while so many others are left standing still? Why is it that some are so resilient and able to persevere while others slip backward?

The difference can be summed up in six words: "They ask for what they need." These business owners are not afraid to learn new effective work practices, enhance their skills, and create dynamic, motivated, and effective teams. They are confident in their knowledge and expertise, yet they recognize their limitations.

Successful franchisees motivate themselves, raise the bar, and most importantly, know how to retain highly effective employees. Startup new franchisees, in particular, recognize that keeping top performers is critical to establishing the foundation necessary to grow and succeed. Employee turnover is expensive and extremely time-consuming, which directly affects team morale, customer service, and profit.

If you plan to thrive, you should make the following practices part of your franchisee's culture:
- Develop a thorough business plan and review/revise frequently.
- Have well-written business mission and vision statements.
- Know your niche market(s) and ideal client(s) and market accordingly.
- Develop a structured orientation program with a team-welcoming rally.
- Define the specific components (DNA) of your business:
  - Be sure all facets of the business are in line with the DNA.
  - Select employees who fit well with the business DNA.
- Create mentor programs.
- Encourage and recognize employees who tap their skills and talents to stretch beyond the scope of their specific job description when appropriate.
- Support ongoing professional development opportunities.
- Establish clearly defined job descriptions and standards by which staff will be appraised.
- Implement routinely scheduled employee performance reviews and use them to mentor personal and professional growth.
- Maintain continual interactive communication with employees.
- Take time to get to know employees and learn about their special interests, talents, abilities, skills, and aspirations.
- Acknowledge special initiatives or accomplishments in the presence of co-workers. Do not underestimate the value of recognition and even a simple thank you.

- Personally attend seminars and workshops focusing on enhancing your leadership skills, staying current with advancements in your industry.
- Be truthful to yourself: Know what you know and seek professional services or hire professionals to advise you or assume the responsibility for what you don't know well.

The key to a thriving business is the owner and employees' continual learning; exploration and development of new programs and services; exceptional customer service; and the ability to keep employees so actively engaged in their jobs—and aligned with the business's mission and goals—that they have no desire to seek greener pastures.

Seek Opportunities to Fail

Typically, we do not think about all the benefits of failure. We would rather deny or not think about failure at all. As business owners, we don't like to fail and certainly don't want to discuss it. Unfortunately, we have come to believe and in some cases are taught that failure is unacceptable, but it is our failures that fuel creativity and innovation and motivation for better things, personal growth, and business success.

Smart business owners learn this lesson early in life and tend to be more visionary, adventurous, and risk-taking and bounce back quickly from failures. They are not afraid to think outside the box, often do not see a box, experiment with new products and services, and venture out to new niche markets.

At its core, failure builds and enhances our self-confidence, character, and perseverance. Years ago, I met a very successful businessman, and I asked about his secret to success. His reply? "I sought out opportunities to fail." I thought I had heard him incorrectly. "Don't you mean opportunities to succeed?" He looked at me and smiled. "If I only sought opportunities I would succeed at, I would have tried very few things. By trying and failing, I learned to fine-tune my business skills, what I really don't know about business, and hired professionals to help take my business to the next level, which resulted in surpassing my competitors."

Business owners who seek opportunities to fail learn to see their failures as learning lessons—stepping stones to success. They recognize that a failure wasn't so bad, and as Elton John puts it, "I'm still standing." They step back and invest the time to evaluate, revise their approach, and go at it again. Individuals who look at failure negatively often say, "I can't do it" and "I'm not going to try that again," and later complain that they are left in the dust of their competitors.

Failing does more than simply build perseverance and confidence; it teaches creative thinking, practical business skills, and teamwork. Having business practices, products, or services fail teaches us to think before we react, question the decisions we are making, and be open to asking for feedback from employees and customers to minimize future failures.

Failure teaches you how to dodge mistakes. We learn what went wrong, and this allows us to identify our mistakes. Most opportunities and challenges we face aren't once-in-a-lifetime. The benefit of failure is that it teaches us how to avoid making the same mistake in the future.

Failure makes you more credible. Embracing and sharing our stories of failure make us more vulnerable. It positions us as seasoned veterans, and when we are talking with investors, customers, or other business owners, it is these failures and the lessons learned that are most highly valued and make us more relatable, which adds to our credibility.

Remember to seek opportunities to fail and do so often. Selecting only those situations you know you will succeed at will limit what you explore. Failure is a valuable stepping stone to business success.

Are You Doing the Right Things the Right Way?

Recently, while I was working with a coaching client, he questioned the efficiency of his daily business operations. The conversation gradually shifted to whether he was actually doing the right things and doing them the right way to effectively increase productivity, grow his business, and be profitable.

We identified the following actions business owners should be taking and how to do them right.

Goals

Establishing goals is easy, but are they measurable, well-documented, and communicated clearly to your employees and management team? When employees fail to achieve set goals, it is generally directly related to the employer's inability to clearly outline expectations and assignments. Taking the time to document writing and communicating goals routinely with the team will clarify expectations, resulting in decreased conflicts and increased performance.

Accountability

Sam Silverstein says in his book, *No More Excuses*, "Accountability is keeping your commitments to people. When you are effective, you do the right things consistently. Every activity you engage in should have a purpose in your quest to keep your commitments and be accountable to the people in your life." Business owners need to be accountable to their employees, customers, and relationships in their business. If they aren't, employees are likely to gradually do less and less, knowing that accountability isn't valued in their organization. In addition, key productive employees may seek alternative employment where they are in the company of competent, responsible owners and employees.

Workforce

Hire the right people for the right positions and quickly fire those who are the wrong fit. You generally know within 30 days if an employee is not cut out for your business. Individuals who are unwilling to take ownership of their poor performance and attitude and are not receptive to correcting negative behavior will negatively affect morale and inhibit the growth of your business. Hiring to quickly fill a seat is never a good idea. There are plenty of talented, productive, and trainable employees to fill your workforce. Set clear job descriptions and expectations and be patient. In time, you will attract ideal prospects.

Integrity

Establish and model your business's DNA of adhering to moral and ethical principles, sound moral character, and honesty. Hiring the right people who are a fit should help eliminate your apprehension to trust, share key information, and delegate tasks. This will instill within your employees a belief that they are trusted to conduct and conform to the accepted standards of right and wrong and take full responsibility for their actions.

Consistency

Being consistent when handling and adhering to your business policies regarding poor performance, tardiness, etc., in a positive and professional manner is vital to ensure productivity and positive employee morale. Employees who consistently fail to meet standards, are not held accountable, and do not have corrective actions imposed on them will eventually cause a dissension among the workforce. Productive, committed employees will begin to question your authority, will see you as a pushover, and may follow suit, becoming slackers or, worse yet, seeking other employment.

Take the time to think about and work on your business. Focusing on these and other facets of business will help you enhance your ability to make the right decisions and do things the right way. In the long run, you will increase employee and customer satisfaction, productivity, and profitability.

Accelerating Your Business

What do you really want to accomplish? Generally, the response has been to have a successful business, become financially secure, and leave an impact on the world—a challenge not easy to accomplish, otherwise everyone would leave a full-time job and jump into the business world.

It requires countless hours of work, risk-taking, financial investment, hiring the right employees, and working with consultants and coaches. Those who rise to the challenge and beat the odds have invested in learning practical habits to navigate through the minefields that have destroyed so many other businesses.

Here are several things most fail to do routinely but should. With determination, consistent focus, time, and these tendencies, you will likely be successful in all facets of your personal life and business.

Dance to a Different Drummer

Top achievers are not afraid to be creative and stand out from the crowd. They embrace making hard decisions, knowing there are risks but that they can lead to major strides and rewards.

Mental and Physical Health

Invest time and money in your personal health needs to be a top priority if you want to maintain the stamina to be effective. The most energetic individuals make no excuses and are committed to caring about their mind and body by eating well, exercising, and socializing and participating in recreational activities.

Be Current and Always Be a Student Eager to Learn

It seems most have endless reasons for not having the time to read or attend seminars, conferences, or workshops. To continue to grow a successful business, it is essential that you stay current. Those who excel designate specific, regularly scheduled time for personal and business development.

Establish a Wisdom Circle

It is said that "birds of a feather flock together," and we are a combination of those we spend most of our time with. So, it makes sense to be selective, network, and surround yourself with grounded, successful, visionary individuals who can fuel your motivation, offer advice, and take your business to the next level.

Be Persistent

Persistence isn't a word you would likely hear discussed at a networking or business meeting. Pushing and motivating yourself consistently is easily said but can be extremely difficult and challenging to implement and maintain. Success comes to people who invest in consistently working hard and working smart on their skills, products, and services.

Set Goals

Business owners often state they have set goals and a business plan and yet, when probed, admit goals are not actually documented with a plan of action or accountability system established, and if they have a business plan, it hasn't been looked at from the day it was written. Those who set specific measurable goals tend to be more productive and focused in their efforts to accomplish the goals and are frequently reviewing, updating, and seeking outside services when needed to reach a higher level of productivity, resulting in greater success.

Internal Audit

Routinely take time to acknowledge your abilities, inabilities, and needs. The most successful business owners are constantly striving to adapt, learn, and hire experts to grow their business. This is not for the weakhearted or those with strong egos; it takes allowing yourself to let your guard down and be vulnerable and trusting.

These tendencies, although easy to establish, take long-term consistent effort, ongoing commitment, and investment of time to grow a successful business, become financially secure, and leave an impact on the world.

What Are You Afraid Of? Delegating Can Set You Free!

Business owners in general either dread or resist delegating tasks and responsibilities to others. The most common excuses are "I want things done my way" and "It takes too long to explain or teach what I want done." Yet when the issue is probed further, at its core is their reluctance and fear to relinquish control.

The ability to delegate sets today's effective business owners apart from the pack. They realize not only that it is necessary to cross-train employees, but also that the need to delegate tasks and responsibilities is essential in light of today's downsized organizations.

Set yourself free by doing the following:
- Select the right person for the right task or responsibility. Take the time to assess an individual's ability and ambition rather than choosing a person at random or abruptly when in

crisis. If this is done well, the individual will feel respected and appreciated and will likely quickly rally and embrace the challenge. If no one in your workforce is ideal for the task, select someone with potential and offer training and mentoring support.
- Be willing to relinquish authority but expect accountability. The most common mistake is to delegate a task or responsibility but limit or restrict the person's authority to make decisions or the freedom to handle tasks differently. If you select the right person or train someone well, you need to be trusting and allow the person to take charge and do his or her job. To ease your anxiety, implement progress review meetings to monitor the person's ability and quality of the assigned duties.
- Take time to adequately explain the specifics of the tasks and your expectations. This can be either verbally or in writing; in some cases, it may be necessary to do both. To minimize the learning curve, it is best to address initial questions and requested needs promptly and thoroughly before handing over the task.
- Jointly, agree on the time frame for the completed project or, if it is an ongoing responsibility, the desired frequency and dates for progress reports.
- Allow the individual to take the initiative to suggest and implement changes to enhance performance, meet deadlines, and be accountable for the quality of work performed. Embrace and compliment the new ways tasks are being completed; avoid pointing fingers and being harsh when alternative ways fail; and offer opportunities to process, learn, and make corrections to move forward.

- Be accessible to review performance and coach to further enhance the individual's abilities. Recognize that when teaching or assigning a new task, it is necessary to be patient and acknowledge there is a learning curve. Coaching can also provide additional insight into a person's ability, which may lead to determining whether you can delegate additional tasks and responsibilities.

Once you have tested the water and recognize the benefit of freeing yourself from tasks and responsibilities, you can focus more on growing your business. In time, you may identify other tasks and responsibilities that can be done by members of your workforce once they are trained.

In the end, everyone benefits: You set yourself free to do what you do best—building the business—while offering employees new opportunities and, in turn, creating a workforce that is more motivated, enhanced, and engaged.

Leadership vs. Management — Do You Recognize the Difference?

Business owners tend to view management and leadership as one and the same when they are actually very different.

To be an effective, successful business owner, you need to acquire both management and leadership skills. Knowing and demonstrating the difference between them is key to being respected by your employees, clients, and vendors.

As the franchisee, you *manage* your finances and you *lead* your workforce. Those who know and demonstrate the difference are in the best position to motivate, coach, and inspire their employees and grow their business.

Here are a few causes that contribute to the confusion between managing and leading in a corporation, business, or association. The most common mistake is to applaud and recognize key productive, engaged, motivated employees or those who have been with the company for an extended period with a promotion to a managerial position and then later find them to be inadequate leaders as well as less happy and engaged. In other cases, it may be the employee with the highest sales record, fewer days absent, or fewer accidents or customer complaints who is rewarded with a promotion.

To effectively manage is to routinely monitor, identify, evaluate, and make positive changes to effectively improve policies and procedures and to explain and train employees to adapt to the changes with the least amount of resistance and disruption while maintaining extraordinary customer service.

Leadership, unlike management, is about leading people rather than dealing with policies and procedures. The following four basic aspects of an effective leader establish the foundation for creating a solid, engaged, and productive workforce, which will help increase productivity and profitability:

1. **Recruitment.** Be the company that is hunted because of your reputation for investing in your employees. Employee turnover is not only time-consuming but also extremely costly. Attracting and retaining the best employees is essential if a company desires to grow and stay competitive. Employees want to have involved bosses who are available

when needed for guidance but otherwise want to be left alone to do their jobs.

2. **"We" culture.** Creating and maintaining a working environment that rewards employees who take risks, strive to enhance their skills, and appreciate the contributions of all employees from the maintenance personnel to the clerical/tech staff to the CEO can only lead to a desired great place to work. Happy, appreciated employees will openly serve as ideal ambassadors who brag about the company throughout the community, which can ultimately result in attracting the best prospective employees and new customers.

3. **Coaching.** Invest the time and energy to really know your employees' interests and abilities and establish routine meetings to motivate and mentor them. Tapping into their total person and offering positive feedback and constructive criticism will enhance skills and could identify potential future leaders. Every employee is different and requires a different approach to stay engaged, motivated, and hungry to improve.

4. **Training.** Investing in training for all employees is imperative to the success of a company and an ideal opportunity for leaders to share their vision, knowledge, and expertise. Allocating the funds yearly for ongoing employee and leadership development training demonstrates the leader's interest in the personal growth of their employees and the growth and profitability of the company—a win-win.

Leaders who learn and embrace these foundational skills and strive to enhance their ability will continue to attract, recruit, and retain the best employees and not be saddled with marginal lackluster employees.

Communicating with Impact Makes a Difference

Employees frequently list ineffective employers and poor communication as the top reasons for leaving. Employees feel there is a lack of quality and quantity of communication of pertinent information regarding the financial stability of the business, challenges, and changes that directly or indirectly affect them.

Employees share that the owner typically gives lip service or minimal information and feels that is sufficient without really communicating. It isn't sufficient to rely only on notices on bulletin boards, emails, memos, and slips in paychecks to disseminate adequate information.

Ineffective and infrequent communication throughout the workforce often results in negative talk and dissemination of inaccurate information that spreads like wildfire. The byproducts can be the departure of employees, decreases in morale and productivity, and negative talk bleeding to the communities and customers served, seriously impacting production and profits.

Patrick Donadio, executive coach/speaker, and author of *Communicating with IMPACT*, says, "In order for leaders to build deeper relationships, they should communicate with employees in three ways: physically, mentally, emotionally. Don't just share information; think of how you can ask open-ended questions to get people to mentally engage and use compelling stories to help them to connect emotionally with you and the organization's mission."

Here are a few ways franchisees can improve personal and business communication:

- **Be approachable.** Don't simply say you have an open-door policy. Make it a practice to walk throughout the company interacting with employees, making you visible and accessible.
- **Be attentive.** Effective communication is a two-way street. It is not simply the sharing of information but also an opportunity to elicit questions, encouraging feedback and suggestions.
- **Give feedback.** When questions are asked or a concern is shared, acknowledge you understand and will investigate. Then be accountable to respond in a timely manner.
- **Ask, ask, and ask.** Don't assume employees understand the instructions or information given. Lack of verbal or nonverbal affirmation does not ensure they comprehended the specifics. Request a verbal response to confirm understanding. Most vagueness is caused by lack of specifics or unfamiliar terminology.
- **Sharing is unifying.** Adopt the mindset that the sharing of information throughout the ranks is providing a service to employees and not a position of power.
- **Make one-on-one and small-group contacts.** In addition to memos, posted notices, and meeting minutes, personal contact with individuals or small groups will help cement the understanding and adoption of changes and information. This will likely minimize delays and errors.
- **Be present and listen.** Give your total attention to the person you're speaking with. It is not only being respectful but also helps create a "we culture" where everyone's opinions and

concerns are viewed equally. Employees who are recognized feel valued and in turn will be more motivated, dedicated, and productive.

Adopting these basic tips will not only create a "we culture" but, more important, position you as a leader who is credible and supportive. Establishing a workplace that is built on trust, respect, and openness is paramount to effective working practices, motivated and engaged employees, and maximized efforts from the entire workforce.

What Makes an Exceptional Manager/Supervisor?

Poor performance is a common problem that negatively affects business owners and employees. Troubled employees may tend to be routinely late or absent, unfit to work, or inefficient or have many ongoing conflicts with fellow employees. Poor performance is also often a result of various personal nonwork-related issues, drug and alcohol abuse or dependency, ongoing debt, compulsive behavior such as gambling, or sudden crises, to name a few. Employees may assist with other employees' poor performance, but it is chiefly the role of managers and owners to identify and solve poor performance problems.

So, it is imperative that business owners hire managers and supervisors who have and demonstrate effective managerial skills. Their responsibility is to manage the employees so that the workforce comfortably and consistently meets the goals of the company and feels valued for its contribution to success. So, what should business owners expect from their managers and supervisors?

Exceptional managers:

- State work expectations and policies directly, consistently, and clearly.
- Routinely observe and document both positive and poor job performance.
- Keep morale high by treating everyone fairly and setting realistic goals.
- Identify and understand troubled employees without losing objectivity.
- Talk with employees about poor performance in a timely manner.
- Consistently give feedback on performance according to established company standards.
- Identify signs of poor performance and possible personal or medical problems (avoiding diagnosing).

Poor performance includes:

- Unsafe behavior: careless, easily distracted, ignores safety rules
- Erratic performance: unreliable, swings between very high and low productivity
- Unfit for work: regularly arrives appearing tired, nervous, irritable, or has mood swings
- Attendance: often late; records indicate frequently absent on Mondays, Fridays, or the day after payday
- Poor judgment: makes foolish decisions or incorrect statements or alters procedures

Personal and medical issues include:

- Chemical or drug abuse or dependency

- Ongoing pressures: legal, financial, or interpersonal problems that may be related to divorce, custody battles, unexpected expenses, or poor financial planning
- Compulsive behavior: eating disorders, gambling, gaming, and compulsive shopping
- Mental health: mood shifts from high to low quickly, depressed, highly anxious, reactive, isolated from others, to name a few

Roles of an Exceptional Manager/Supervisor
- **Role model:** An effective manager influences the workforce by setting an example with an overall positive attitude, treats everyone with respect, and values everyone's contribution equally.
- **Link:** Managers are the communication link between the business owner and the workforce. They have the ability to be the voice of the employees and share their needs and concerns. They must also consistently communicate the company's standards, policies, and mission.
- **Leader:** They manage all facets of the workflow, meeting schedules, resources, and meeting production standards.
- **Evaluator:** Managers should evaluate each employee's job performance in a timely fashion, using the company's standard evaluation form objectively, and avoid diagnosing personal or medical issues.

With these skills and experience, managers can bring out the best in their employees and themselves and create a powerful, productive workforce.

Effective Communication Takes an Open Mind, Patience, and Tolerance

Let's face it: Effective communication is incredibly important in all facets of our lives. As you are well aware, not everyone communicates or participates in conversations in the same way. This can negatively impact the outcome of meetings, negotiations, family disputes, and daily interactions with customers, colleagues, and the general public.

These different approaches or styles of communicating are so different that it is no wonder misunderstandings and conflicts often occur. Having an understanding of another individual's thought process, feelings, and experiences requires taking a moment to relate to their personal frame of reference. With this basic understanding, it is imperative that we continually maintain an open mind and be tolerant and inclusive, remembering that communication is a two-way process and that this results in positive, productive outcomes. Let's discuss different types of communicators.

Investors are those individuals who are interested and actively engaged in the discussion. They are likely to ask questions while trying to relate to and understand the points of view of others. They tend to be the group mediator if the discussion gets out of hand and serve as the translator, often offering a repackage of an apparent misunderstood comment made by others. Investors contribute comments like, "Am I correct in understanding what you mean, that you think the best course of action is...?" or "I believe Mark's comment is in line with the comment made by Karen earlier."

Analyzers or **thinkers** are individuals who are typically quiet and often overlooked. They are actively listening and observing until they have the full picture of the issue at hand. When they have digested the information and feel comfortable, they will ask a few probing, well-crafted questions. Once it is apparent the questions are well received, they will offer more detailed feedback and explanations of their opinions and suggestions. Analyzers may make a comment like, "Does it sound reasonable…?" or "Could this be what's going on…?"

Ambassadors, by contrast, tend to set the tone of the interaction and communicate more often than most throughout a meeting. They tend to interject jokes and could drift frequently from topic to topic. They can consume vital time if not redirected. However, they can also be effective in drawing in all participants to a conversation.

Then there are those **take-charge** individuals who like to control and direct all communication. Typically, they take the reins of a conversation or meeting by communicating in short, blunt, task-oriented comments at the start to set the interaction in motion. Unlike the others, they are concerned about the details, having a clear agenda, and keeping the discussion on track and on time.

So, if you really want to be an effective communicator and minimize conflicts, misunderstandings, and stalemates, invest time in listening to and observing how others communicate. Encouraging and respecting the different styles of communicating will maximize the sharing of key solutions and needed feedback, resulting in positive outcomes.

CHAPTER 12 –

National Marketing vs. Local Marketing

By Lynne Shelton

What to Expect

I get asked a lot of questions around national marketing versus local marketing from both franchisors and franchisees alike. You should think of national marketing as "brand building" not geared toward any particular business or location, while local marketing is marketing that is done to highlight a particular location within the franchise system.

Most prospective franchisees want to know why they should contribute to a national marketing fund, especially in smaller franchise systems that may not be "national" yet. Usually, those franchisors use the national marketing fund in a regional way, meaning that they focus only on where they have franchise locations or will soon have locations opening. It is to build brand awareness to consumers about the benefits of your brand. Although not always directly attributable to the specific location, it will bring in customers to your business over time.

Local marketing or advertising (depending on whether it is allowed in your franchise agreement) could include things like promotional events; outreach activity support; elementary, junior high, high school, or college sponsorships; media days; "Register to win" contests; social media postings, creating landing pages; local charity partnerships; friends and family events; and traditional advertising—print collateral, magazine ads, specific housing community ads, and door hangers.

How Much Should You Spend?

The second question I always get asked is how much to spend on marketing the business. In the case of the national marketing, that amount will be dictated by your franchise agreement. This amount can change over time if your franchise agreement allows it to, although it is usually capped, adding a certain percentage increase per year or during the term of your agreement. Common amounts are 1% to 2% of gross sales.

Although it is true that it is on the franchisor to determine how to spend the budget, you should see that it is focused on building the brand.

Remember the days when brand loyalty grew year by year? Today's most successful brands of consumer goods were built by heavy advertising and marketing investments long ago. But recently, many marketers have lost sight of the connection between advertising spending and market share. They seem to practice the art of discounting: cutting ad budgets to fund price promotions or fatten quarterly earnings. They may win the volume battle today, but they will lose the competitive war.

We must remember that brand value and consumer preference for brands drive market share. Most important, good franchisors must understand the balance of advertising and promotion expenditures needed to build brands and gain share, market by market, regardless of growth trends in the product categories where they compete.

We can look at some examples from food manufacturers that we are all familiar with to see how this has worked. Procter & Gamble, for example, has built its Jif and Folger's brands from single-digit shares to category leaders. In peanut butter and coffee, P&G invests more in advertising and less in discounting than its major competitors. Kellogg and General Mills, waging an escalating ad-spending war in breakfast cereals, together now command 65% of the market—and their stock trades at much higher valuations than other food companies. Coke and Pepsi invest so much in advertising that they make it cost-prohibitive for anyone else to compete with them. Together they own 70% of the market.

What do these great marketers have in common? Among other things, awareness of a key factor in advertising: consistent advertising spending. They do not minimize their budgets to raise earnings up for a few quarters. They know that advertising should not be managed as a discretionary cost but a required cost of doing business.

Harvard business experts have consistently reported that if individual business owners open to the public (business-to-consumer businesses) want to quickly grow their business, they should be spending a total of 15% of gross sales per year on all forms of advertising. For a moderate growth rate, a business should spend 10% of gross sales, and to maintain market share, a business owner needs to spend at least 4% of their gross sales. For businesses that are not open to the public (business-to-business companies) should spend anywhere from 1.4% to 2.5% at a minimum of gross sales to keep their business with its current market share and 8% to 15% for moderate growth. Many experts think it actually takes a higher percentage for business-to-business advertising than for business-to-consumer companies, although admittedly the type of advertising done can be very different.

No matter what type of business you are running, the percentages of advertising do not always include just dollars spent. Advertising could include items such as free coffee for all firefighters, police, and other first responders, or sponsoring a Little League T-ball team in your local town that your child plays on, or even sponsoring a nonprofit event that captures your heart. You can include the amount of dollars it costs to obtain that advertising and count it toward your local advertising budget spent.

Most franchise agreements require you to notify the franchisor of all forms of local advertising that you do. Make sure that you include the tangible and intangible marketing that you are doing as your full cost spent on local advertising. Additionally, keep track of these items yourself and track the outcome, so you can be sure of what customers come in based on both the tangible and the intangible marketing that you are doing. This will ensure that next year, you can fine-tune the items you're spending your effort on so as to obtain more focused or higher results with your advertising.

CHAPTER 13

During the Term

By Lynne Shelton

Why Should You Stay Excited After Year Four?

Many franchisees begin to wonder around year four, why am I still paying the franchisor all this money to be a part of the franchise system? The fact of all the training and assistance they received is a long-faded memory for most. So why do you continue to pay for the full term? Besides the fact that you signed a legally binding agreement, here is an advance-placed reminder you can come back to when you start feeling that way.

Knowledge
You just think you know it all…

Although you expect the moon from the franchisor, be careful to stay within the procedures within the franchise system. At the beginning of year four, it is common to think that you may know it all, but you will still need the expertise of the franchisor—always.

Benchmarks

The reason most franchisors require you to use specific reports, accounting systems, and POS (place of service) software systems is that all franchisees can be benchmarked. Why would you want to be a part of benchmarking? So that it can be used for one-to-one mentoring. Most franchisors will provide quarterly reviews of your information to ensure that your numbers are within normal ranges with the other franchisees, including on your expenses portion of your Profit & Loss. If your numbers are lower than the benchmarked average, then the franchisor can help you to improve those numbers by giving you tips, sometimes inside tricks of how to accomplish that in each area of your chart of accounts. And if your numbers are higher than the benchmark, you will be able to share with the franchisor representative how you have accomplished that. This information could help other franchisees to improve their bottom line as well. This could even lead to an award at the annual convention.

If your franchise is needing sales or income help, the franchisor can share what you should be selling or producing per quarter/month/year (whatever measure you use). The middle part of the Profit & Loss is usually more under control of the franchisor. The Cost of Goods should be more stable due to arranged, approved suppliers and bargaining vendor agreements. If your franchisor is not focused on reducing the costs of all the required items that franchisees must purchase for the brand, make sure you help them to focus on it, as its importance is paramount.

Most brands today, around 65%, have an Item 19 in their Franchise Disclosure Document. Item 19, the Financial Performance Representations, is what prospective franchisees use to see how much money they can make by reviewing how much other franchise owners are making. Although Item 19 does not have to include sales figures by law, most do at some level. This information could also include typical franchisee costs and average sales, as far as number of customers handled or product numbers sold. No matter which way the information is shown, it can be used by you to create your own benchmarks and goals. You can carry this over to your franchise year after year. Who do you want to emulate in your business? Which factors do you think are most important to track? Is it the number of customers being served, the market share you have in your local market, or the total sales volume you achieved? Share this information with your team, so they also know what is important to you.

Vendors and Suppliers

Most franchisors will also continue providing assistance with the suppliers and vendors. If you are approached by a potential new supplier of required products who would be able to service all franchisees effectively and efficiently, make sure you share that information with the franchisor. Many franchise systems have a mechanism to report such data, although most franchisors will also require you to pay a fee or provide, at minimum, specific information or even a sample or specimen along with the submission to minimize the evaluation period from the franchisor's perspective. They will usually put the vendor through an evaluation as well. They must make sure that the vendor will be able to perform at least as good as the previous vendor did. They could evaluate things such as growth ability and desire, quality control, customer service aspects, distribution channels already in place, and the ability for just-in-time deliveries in addition to pricing.

Although for your and your staff's peace of mind, I do recommend that "No solicitation" signs be hung in your location to avoid as many vendor solicitors as possible. Once you open your business to the public, you will go on all kinds of lists; whether phone, telemarketing, mail marketing, or door-to-door salespeople, it can get quite exhausting to speak to, turn away, or weed through all those vendors. Therefore, it is important to turn over any that you feel are great for the franchise system as a whole to the franchisor; it helps keep other franchisees from going through this at their location.

Competition

Additionally, the franchisor will assist you in knowing how to combat competitors as they inevitably pop up in your area. The more successful you are, the more competitors you will most likely have. Success often begins at the beginning of your relationship when evaluating leases. A lot of franchisors will ensure that you have exclusive right to your area of trade within a complex, shopping center, or geographical area.

Knowledge can continue at the annual conventions. Oftentimes these conventions will include information about what your competitors are doing, advertising or marketing tricks that are working, as well as ways that the brand intends to use for increasing the market share for the upcoming terms.

What Should Happen in Year Nine?

Year nine is a pivotal year. Typically, it is the year that you will be deciding whether to renew your franchise agreement for another term. Most franchise agreements are a 10-year term, although that's not always the case; you can say that a year or two before the end of your franchise agreement will always be a pivotal year for you. You should review your return on investment. In this review, include all of your initial costs as well as any upkeep or refreshing you've done during the period of your franchise agreement. Then evaluate that against the sales and the net profit that you have achieved. It is best if, when looking at these figures, you remove any amounts that you paid yourself or any other benefits that you have given yourself or your family through the business. This will ensure that you're looking at a clean return on investment, not just expenditure versus net profit. This will help you make the decision whether to renew your franchise agreement or exit the system as a lesson learned.

CHAPTER 14

The Renewal

By Lynne Shelton

You will need to notify your franchisor usually around nine months to a year before the end of your term whether you will be renewing your franchise agreement. This enables them to attempt to locate another franchisee for your territory if you are choosing to exit the system. If you're allowed to sell your business, then this would also be the time to start marketing it for sale, to give you the best opportunity to sell it before the franchise agreement ends. Once the franchise agreement term comes to an end, you have no legal right to still have the franchise business, and it will most certainly be terminated and could even become the franchisor's business. You will find out whether you have the right to renew the franchise agreement by looking in the FDD in Item 17.

Choosing Nonrenewal

If you choose not to renew, there are specific steps you will need to take based on the executed franchise agreement you signed.

In addition to following the items listed in the Termination section of your franchise agreement, you may be asked to do an Exit interview. These can include questions such as:

1. What network drive/cloud drive (Box/Dropbox) have you been using?

2. What personal email address did you use to send emails to yourself to do work later, etc.?
3. What passwords are associated with the cloud drive, IM accounts, email account, etc.?
4. Where are the communications stored?

You will also be reminded of the executed Nondisclosure of Trade Secret obligations and Noncompete provisions, if they are present in the franchise agreement you signed, for the owners, partners, managers, or individuals. And they most likely are. Typically, all signers, owners, and potential guarantors of the franchise unit will have a noncompete provision that lasts at least two years after the termination of the franchise agreement. It will also likely contain a provision that places the noncompetition within a radius around the location of your franchise, such as "within 20 miles of the Territory." The provision could also commonly be more restrictive, adding "within 20 miles of the Territory, or within 20 miles of any Franchisee's Territory at the time of Termination." This means that not only can you not open a competing business within 20 miles of where your franchise was located, but you also cannot move across the country and be within 20 miles of any franchisee's location for two years. Obviously, this is for the protection of the entire franchise brand, and if you are choosing to renew and stay with the franchise system, this is a good way to keep very knowledgeable competitors (ex-franchisees) out of your Territory.

Choosing Renewal

If you choose to renew your franchise agreement, there are several things you should do.

Location

The first thing you and your franchisor should determine together is whether to keep the business where it is currently located. Most franchisors that have franchises open to the public will have a real estate division or system to assist you with this. You need to evaluate things such as the demographics of your location currently as compared to how they were when you began at that location. Additionally, ensure that they are evaluating the psychographics where your buyers are to ensure that they have not left the driving range to your location. You could have the most beautiful store, but if your buyers aren't coming to it, what good is it to you or the franchisor?

Lease

Once you make sure that the location is one that you want to stay at, you will need to make sure that it is financially desirable as well. At least nine months prior to the end of your franchise agreement, you should begin negotiating the renewal on your lease. In some cases, this outcome may dictate a move of your location. However, after you have successfully negotiated the renewal of your lease, it is time to refresh.

Refresh

After reviewing your return on investment, especially if you decide to move forward with renewal, you should refresh the business if it is open to the public. Many franchise systems also require a refresh. This includes things such as painting and renewing surfaces, which could include new flooring, new chairs or benches, new artwork if allowed by the franchise agreement, or even potentially new signage, if it has become faded or cracked. Since you plan on signing another franchise agreement, renewing your vehicle leases is a great idea, if that is a part of your franchise system. This will keep the brand fresh when the people see you riding around in the vehicles.

The Renewal Franchise Agreement

Make sure that the renewal franchise agreement contains any specially negotiated terms from your first agreement. You may need to rehire the attorney who helped you the first time around, or if you cannot locate them, another franchise attorney could assist. Once you have signed your renewal franchise agreement, then get ready to enjoy your next term. Remember to take all of the same steps that we've mentioned in this book to increase the profitability of your business during your second term. Don't forget to acknowledge what made you successful and to continue that during your second term. Also remember that although it is your business, it is not your brainchild. You did not create the concept, and you did not keep the brand going for all those years—the franchisor did. So, make sure that you stay plugged in with the franchisor and the other franchisees to create the synergy you need to continually improve on yourself and your business. And don't hesitate to continually look at your second agreement's return on investment. What most franchisees find is that the return on investment keeps improving during the second and successive terms.

Conclusion

By Lynne Shelton

It has been our pleasure to discuss the various aspects of buying a franchise during this *Journey to Franchise Ownership*. Owning a business is a dream for many people, and franchising is a great way to experience that dream while still maintaining some protection from those hurdles that new businesses can experience. With the right team and with some self-awareness of strengths, weaknesses, goals, and desires, this dream can become a reality for every person.

We wish you luck in your franchise relationships. Good luck in starting the franchise of your choice; the franchise industry is a fantastic collaborative family.

We hope this book was helpful in making the decision to become a franchisee. And if you made the decision to become a franchisee, we hope that this book will lead you into many successful years within the franchise family. If you choose to become a franchisee after reading our book, we would love to hear from you. Email us at processing@sla.law, or leave us a review where you bought the book.

Just like franchisors, we are always open to hearing from you about any ideas of desired content or topics that you wish the book would have covered or any areas that you wish we would have gone into more depth on. As it is said, "iron sharpens iron"; all of us can only become better when each of us makes the others sharper. Good luck to you, your family, your staff, and your business.

God Bless and Happy Franchising!

APPENDIX

23 Items Required in the FDD

Item 1: The Franchisor, and Any Parents, Predecessors, and Affiliates
Item 2: Business Experience
Item 3: Litigation
Item 4: Bankruptcy
Item 5: Initial Fees
Item 6: Other Fees
Item 7: Estimated Initial Investment
Item 8: Restrictions on Sources of Products and Services
Item 9: Franchisee's Obligations
Item 10: Financing
Item 11: Franchisor's Assistance, Advertising, Computer Systems, and Training
Item 12: Territory
Item 13: Trademarks
Item 14: Patents, Copyrights, and Proprietary Information
Item 15: Obligation to Participate in the Actual Operation of the Franchise Business
Item 16: Restrictions on What the Franchisee May Sell
Item 17: Renewal, Termination, Transfer, and Dispute Resolution
Item 18: Public Figures
Item 19: Financial Performance Representations
Item 20: Outlets and Franchisee Information
Item 21: Financial Statements

Item 22: Contracts
Item 23: Receipt

ABOUT THE AUTHORS

Lynne D. Shelton, Esq.
Shelton Law & Associates

Ms. Shelton was the COO of a large franchise system and is currently the Senior Attorney for Shelton Law & Associates franchise law firm, as well as a franchisor owner in an international franchise system.

Ms. Shelton has been counseling Franchise/Business Opportunity clients for over 30 years. She especially enjoys working with small business owners assisting them to "Expand their Brand®."

Since starting the law firm, she has been focused on providing the "Missing Piece" with legal services to small and emerging businesses. Her business savviness combined with her belief in mentorship is the backbone of the law firms slogan, "Your Outsourced In-house Counsel".

Ms. Shelton focuses on ensuring clients are offered individualized service while handling Franchise Disclosures, registrations, legal creation, leases, trusts and vendor distributions within a clients business.

Ms. Shelton has published many articles and has even written books. She has been married for over 30 yrs. and has one son and a sponsored daughter from Haiti. In her spare time she is the CEO of a Non-Profit, Raising a Nation Foundation and teaches leadership development in third world countries to future colleagues and volunteers at her church.

Visit www.LynneShelton.com or http://sla.law/meet-the-team/lynne/

Email me at Lynne@SLA.Law; or in LinkedIn at https://www.linkedin.com/in/lynneshelton/

ABOUT THE AUTHORS

Richard J. Avdoian, CSP™, MS, MSW

Richard Avdoian is the founder and CEO of Midwest Business Institute, Metro St. Louis—a leadership coaching and training group. He is also the founder of the Men Mentoring Men Network in Metro St. Louis.

Mr. Avdoian has worked with franchisees, businesses, corporations, and associations in over 40 industries and is committed to training and retaining highly motivated, productive employees. With programs and services in teamwork, leadership, employee development, and customer service, he enhances employee potential to provide exemplary customer service and increase productivity and profitability.

Nationally known as a high-energy speaker offering keynotes, seminars, and workshops that inspire, inform, and entertain, Mr. Avdoian combines book- and street-smarts to deliver content-rich, high-energy, and innovative, carefully customized presentations. His credentials for employee development and teamwork expertise rank him among the top speakers in the United States and form the foundation for his ability to deliver excellent content material.

In July 2003, Mr. Avdoian received the international designation of Certified Speaking Professional (C.S.P.) from the National Speakers Association (NSA), the highest level of excellence attainable in the industry that only about 17 percent of NSA members worldwide have earned.

He's authored numerous articles for various publications and has been a frequent guest on business radio stations and national and international podcasts. His monthly column, "Smart Business," was featured in the St. Louis Small Business Monthly for several years. In addition, Mr. Avdoian has authored several books, including *Smart Business: Effective Practices for Business Success*, and his book, *Successfully Working Trade Shows: Practical Tips to Attract New Clients, Strengthen Your Brand, and Make More Sales*.

Clients include Mr. Appliance, National Association of Postal Supervisors, American Bankers Association, Corning Glass Company, Peabody Coal Company, Associated General Contractors of America, Monsanto, Illinois City Management Association, United Meat Cutters Union, United States Air Force and Meeting Professionals International. He has also provided counsel to franchisees from State Farm, Mr. Appliance, and McDonald's.

If you want to invite Richard to speak or present to your company, franchise, corporation, or association or learn more about his programs and services, visit www.RichardAvdoian.com, Richard@RichardAvdoian.com, https://www.linkedin.com/in/richardavdoian/.

www.ingramcontent.com/pod-product-compliance
Ingram Content Group UK Ltd.
Pitfield, Milton Keynes, MK11 3LW, UK
UKHW021325180426
11947UKWH00017B/1441